D0462389

Topics in Autism

A Picture's Worth

PECS and Other Visual Communication Strategies in Autism

Andy Bondy, Ph.D., &
Lori Frost, M.S., CCC/SLP

Woodbine House ◆ 2001

© Woodbine House 2002

All rights reserved under International and Pan-American copyright conventions. Published in the United States of America by Woodbine House, Inc., 6510 Bells Mill Road, Bethesda, MD 20817. 800-843-7323. www.woodbinehouse.com

Library of Congress Cataloging-in-Publication Data

Bondy, Andy.
  A picture's worth : PECS and other visual communication strategies in autism / Andy Bondy & Lori Frost.—1st ed.
      p. cm.— (Topics in autism)
  Includes bibliographical references and index.
  ISBN 0-933149-96-4 (pbk.)
  1. Autistic children. 2. Autistic children—Rehabilitation. 3. Interpersonal communication. I. Frost, Lori. II. Title. III. Series.

RJ506.A9 B655 2002
618.92'898203—dc21

                                                        2001046790

Manufactured in the United States of America

First edition
10   9   8   7   6   5   4   3   2   1

This book is dedicated to my father,
Harry L. Bondy,
my first—and best—teacher.
Andy

TABLE OF CONTENTS

ACKNOWLEDGEMENTS

We would like to thank the children we've worked and played with over the years for all they have taught us. We thank our own children, Rayna, John, Alexis, and Sam, for their support and tolerance of the adjustments we've had to make to help schools and families far from home. We also thank our parents for becoming parents to our children when we've needed to travel to the far side of the Earth. Our voice can be heard (and our pictures seen) because of the love and astute support of everyone within our Pyramid companies. To them, we extend our appreciation of their dedication to our shared vision and the tremendous collaboration in thought and deed they have shown to us.

INTRODUCTION

I (AB) first learned about Kurt from a friend who worked in the local children's hospital. He told me that staff had worked on developing a type of body armor for this three-year-old boy, complete with helmet, elbow, wrist, and knee guards! I asked why this boy needed so much protection and my friend answered, "Well, it's to protect him from himself!" I had worked with a number of children who hurt themselves, but never one so young. He was scheduled to visit our school the next day.

Kurt's mother, who appeared very caring but apprehensive, brought him to the school. She told us that he did not speak, and although there were many things he liked, he almost always did them by himself. She started to talk about his "outbursts" while he was quietly sitting on her lap. Suddenly, he made a small noise and leaped out of her lap. Instantly, he was on the floor, slamming his forehead onto the hard tiles. Before I could reach him, he started to run toward the door. I quickly picked him up and he immediately scratched my face and pulled my beard. While still holding him, I turned him around so his hands were further from my face. He responded by kicking backward into my stomach. I put him down, and watched as he jumped up and down on his knees. He then bolted to the door, where he smashed the front of his face into the door. During this entire episode, which lasted no more than a minute, his mother sat quietly, looking as bewildered as all the professionals in the room.

What is the problem here? Kurt was a young boy diagnosed as having autism. He was three years old but had not used speech. Were his problems with communication related to his behavioral difficulties? Were his behavioral difficulties related to his communication problems? Were his communication difficulties only related to the absence of speech, or were the issues even deeper? Finally, what strategies could his mother, family members, and professionals use to best help Kurt?

This book is intended to help parents and professionals understand the communication difficulties of children and adults like Kurt who do not speak, including those with autism spectrum disorders. In the early chapters of this book, we will describe some of the characteristics of people who are nonverbal and provide examples of our approach to understanding communication. We will also describe the relationship between communication and various behavioral difficulties. In the next chapters, we will describe several intervention strategies, including the use of sign language and other less formal gestural systems, and various picture- or symbol-based systems. Included in this review will be a number of low-tech approaches (use of photographs and line drawings) as well as high-tech approaches (use of electronic systems, such as voice-output devices). Throughout this review, we will provide ways to assess whether an approach is appropriate for a particular child or adult. In the last chapters, we will describe various strategies using visual cues to enhance a person's understanding of our instructions, issues associated with learning to wait and deal with transitions, and how such strategies can enhance the effectiveness of different motivational strategies.

Why should we devote an entire book to helping those children who have difficulty acquiring speech to communicate through other means? I think continuing with the story about Kurt will help answer this question.

Kurt started an intense full-time special training program organized within the public schools. First, his teachers figured out what Kurt liked and what could help him pay attention to his surroundings. It was clear that while he needed to learn to imitate what people said and did, he had no such skills on entering the program. Within a few days, Kurt was taught to use the Picture Exchange Communication System (PECS). During the first training session, Kurt learned to calmly give a picture of a pretzel (his favorite treat) to his teacher. This lesson was taught without using any questions from the staff—in fact, Kurt was able to spontaneously give the picture to the teacher when he saw her holding the pretzel. Within a few days, he learned to use single pictures to request other favorite items.

Kurt next learned to put two icons on a card to form a simple sentence. He then learned to clarify some of his requests—communicating that he wanted the BIG pretzel, for example. As he learned new ways to ask for things, he also learned to tell his teachers about simple things in the classroom. During this period of training, his parents used PECS at home to help Kurt communicate with everyone in his family. Both at school and at home, Kurt became much calmer with far fewer tantrums, as he now had an effective, easy system to use to let others know what he wanted.

Many people are afraid that using nonverbal communication systems such as Kurt used makes it less likely that children will learn to talk. We will discuss that point in more detail later, but the simple truth is that there is no evidence that visual systems will interfere with or inhibit the development of speech. In fact, there is growing support that using such systems may have a beneficial impact on speech development. As you can see, Kurt learned to become an effective communicator even though he had not yet learned to speak. But the primary point of this book is **not** to emphasize strategies that will always lead to speech. Instead, this book will focus on ways to help children learn to become effective communicators.

Our emphasis is on helping children learn functional communication skills—that is, the ability to direct behavior to another person in order to receive direct rewards (such as the item they want) or social rewards (such as praise or a pleasant interaction). The table on the next page lists the critical functional communication skills we will focus on.

Critical Functional Communication Skills

Critical Communication Skills USED by the Person	Critical Communication Skills UNDERSTOOD by the Person
Request reinforcers (desired items or activities)	Follow instructions
Ask for help	Follow a schedule
Ask for a break	Wait
Respond "No" to "Do you want . . . ?"	Transitions
Respond "Yes" to "Do you want . . . ?"	Answer questions

When children (and adults) acquire functional communication skills, their lives—and those of their families and teachers—become greatly enriched.

1 | What is Communication?

I worked with Anna from the time she was twenty-six months old. She had big blue eyes and always fixed them on me when I entered the classroom. On the day that we met, I walked over to her and picked her up. She immediately smiled, so I started to slowly spin her around while in my arms. She laughed and tossed her head back. We played this game for several minutes. The next morning when I entered the room, she ran over to me and held her arms up. I waited to see what would happen next. She used no words or even any sounds. But she continued to lift her arms and just about walked on my shoes! Finally, her arms and pleading eyes won me over and I picked her up and spun her around. While she had not spoken, I certainly knew what she wanted!

What is the essence of communication? Is speech necessary for people to communicate? Are there ways to communicate without using speech? These are critical questions for many people without speech. How we answer these questions may have important impacts on the solutions we create and try to implement.

Webster's Collegiate dictionary (1988) defines *communication* as "a process by which information is exchanged between individuals through a common system of symbols, signs, or behavior." That common system is generally referred to as *language*. Language, in turn, can be defined as "a code that we learn to use in order to communicate ideas and express our wants and needs."* Language can be made up of spoken and written words, as the English language is, or can consist of gestures (American Sign Language), symbols alone (Braille), or other codes.

---

* New Jersey Speech-Language Hearing Association website (2001). www.njsha.org.

If you have read reports by speech-language pathologists (SLPs), you probably know that two broad types of language skills are needed in order to communicate:

- *expressive communication* (language): using language to convey messages and
- *receptive communication* (language): understanding the messages from others.

This chapter will focus on using communication skills to convey messages (expressive language), while the next chapter will address understanding the communication of other people (receptive language).

In lay terms, we usually describe communication as an act that conveys an idea or a feeling. In fact, we typically believe that people first have ideas and feelings and then express them via their language. Thus, when we listen to someone speaking, we believe we know about his ideas or feelings. However, if we examine this scenario a little further, it becomes clearer that by listening, we only know about the words spoken. We have no direct connection with the ideas of another person. When you and I speak together, if you don't understand my words, you may ask questions or suggest alternatives. These may bring about a better understanding of what I am saying, but it really does not let you know directly my ideas. When the interaction is between you and a child with a serious communication problem, you will have even less opportunity to probe deeper into what he is thinking or feeling. This type of analysis of behaviors does *not* mean that people do not think, have ideas, or feelings. It only means that we can only know what other people do and say—the rest is speculation and interpretation.

Communicative Behaviors

One of the most effective techniques for teaching communication and other skills to children with autism is a system called *applied behavior analysis.* In the simplest terms, behavior analysis is the study of behavior as it systematically relates to the environment—both events before the behavior (often referred to as *antecedents*) and events happening after the behavior (referred to as *consequences*). For instance, a gust of wind blows a speck of dirt into your child's eye (the antecedent) and he begins to cry (the behavior). He then asks you for a tissue (the behavior) and you quickly give him one (the consequence).

B.F. Skinner, the psychologist who did much of the pioneering work in the field of ABA, taught that all behavior—from simple actions, to complex language (including the actions of children and adults with disabilities)—can be systematically studied. In 1957, Skinner wrote a book describing how different types of communication are systematically related to environmental factors, from items in our surroundings to what other people say to us. While the complete analysis tends to be very complex, an understanding of some of his theories will be very helpful to our ability to help children who have difficulty communicating and using speech.

Analyzing Communication by Its Antecedents and Consequences

A behavior analyst acts much like an investigative reporter. In grade school, we all learned that a good newspaper report not only told us about *what* happened, but also about how, when, where, and why. In behavior analysis, we are interested in what happened (the behavior), but we also want to understand how, when, and where the behavior occurred, as well as why the behavior took place.

What Behavior Is Communication?

If we are to study the behavior of communication, then the first thing we should define is how it is different from other types of behavior. Not all behaviors are communicative, so we must identify what is unique about behaviors that we do call communicative. For example, a child walks into his kitchen, goes to the refrigerator, opens the door, takes out a can of soda, and drinks it. In this case, the child acted on different things in the environment and was reinforced for these actions by drinking the soda. No communication is identified here—the child acted directly on the environment. It is important to note that if you were watching the child (although the child didn't see you), you could interpret his actions with the can of soda to indicate that he was thirsty or that he wanted the soda. However, our ability to interpret his actions does *not* make his actions communicative. We must separate our interpretation from the true reasons for the child's actions—in this case, getting the soda did not involve communication.

Now, let us assume that the child walks into the kitchen, goes over to his mother, and says, "Soda!" His mother goes to the refrigerator, retrieves a can of soda, gives it to her child, and watches as he drinks the soda. In this case, the outcome for the child is the same as in our last example—he ends up drinking the soda. But this time, he directed an action toward his mother—he said, "Soda!" His mother then acted on the environment and assured that he would get the soda. We would all agree that this scenario does involve communication because the child acted toward his mother, instead of the refrigerator.

Why Do We Communicate?

Now let's examine how behaviorists look at the fundamental reasons for communicative behavior—that is, why do we communicate? We will keep our analysis straightforward and look at two examples highlighting the basic reasons to communicate.

In our example about the young boy who walked into the kitchen and asked for soda, he communicated with his mother in order to get a drink. His mother listened to his communication and made sure (as mothers do!) that he got what he wanted. Here we can see that one of the reasons this boy communicates is to get other people to get him things that he wants (that is, to *request*).

Now, let's consider a different situation. Imagine a twenty-month-old girl who is using some single words. She is sitting in the living room looking out the bay window. Suddenly, she says,

"Plane! Plane!" over and over. Why is she saying this? To understand her reason, we must watch what her mother does. It is very unlikely that the girl wants her mother to get the airplane. If we watch, her mother is very likely to say something like, "Yes, it is a plane! I see the plane, too! Look how pretty the plane is!" In this case, the outcome of the child's communication is the social reaction (including mom's words) by her mother. Those of you who have had this type of interaction also recall how persistent the child can be! She may say, "Plane!" over and over until her mother acknowledges her comment. For this young girl, the social outcome is very motivating for her *comments*.

So, we now see two primary reasons to communicate. One reason involves relatively concrete outcomes, such as receiving favorite snacks or toys. The other reason is generally social in nature—the praise or attention that we may receive from commenting about the world around us. (See Chapter 5 for some additional reasons for communication.)

If your child does not have appropriate communication skills, it will be very important to determine which kind of communication you want to teach. Although it may seem equally important to teach requests and comments, we must remember that comments are usually learned due to their social consequences. For children with autism, social consequences are generally not powerful motivators. Thus, early in our intervention, teaching comments may prove very difficult. On the other hand, if you know what your child likes in terms of concrete outcomes, then teaching requesting will have some immediate and powerful effects. We will return to this point when we focus attention on specific communication systems and teaching strategies.

When and Where Do We Communicate?

Peggy was referred to me by her family physician. In her clinical notes were indications that Peggy could speak but was "stubborn" or "lazy." When Peggy and I played, it was clear that she liked to play with a set of little dolls. She reached for the dolls but would not ask for them. If I held onto a doll she would begin to whine. If I said, "Tell me what you want" she quickly said, "doll!" However, if I didn't speak, she didn't speak. In my view, she wasn't stubborn; she simply had not yet learned when to use her words.

To understand when and where we communicate, it is helpful to consider several different situations and see how they influence our views about communication. For example, consider a girl who walks into a room, sees you and a bowl of popcorn, walks over to you and says, "Popcorn!" We would give this child credit for being spontaneous. She initiated the interaction without any assistance from us.

Now consider a girl who sees the same situation but simply stands in front of the bowl of popcorn. We patiently wait but she does not speak. We then ask, "What do you want?" The girl immediately says, "Popcorn!" In this case, we would say that the girl can speak but she needs a prompt or a cue from someone else.

Finally, consider another girl in the same situation who also does not initially speak. When we ask, "What do you want?" the girl says nothing. Then we say, "Popcorn" and the girl immediately says, "Popcorn!" In this case, we would say the child is able to imitate. That is, she may speak but only if she hears a specific model from someone else.

In each of these three situations, the child said the word, "Popcorn." So if we asked the simple question, "Does the child speak?" the answer in all three cases would be, "Yes!" However, each child actually did something different, and it would be misleading to say each response was equivalent to the others. Although the "why" for each girl was the same (that is, they each wanted popcorn), we must interpret what happened differently because the situations leading up to the girls speaking were different. (See Table 1-1.)

At this point, it would be reasonable to think that if a child could say the word "popcorn" then he should be able to use it in each of the five scenarios described. Unfortunately, this transfer does not always happen, not only for children with autism (and other communication difficulties) but also for children acquiring

Table 1-1 | Types of Communication

Setting	Child's Statement	Outcome	Type of Communication
Child sees mom holding a bowl of popcorn	"I want popcorn" or "Popcorn"	Mom gives child	Spontaneous request
Child sees mom holding a bowl of popcorn	"I see popcorn"	Mom says, "Yes, I see the popcorn, too!"	Spontaneous mom comment
Mom says to child, "What do you want?"	"Popcorn"	Mom gives child popcorn	Responsive request
Mom says to child, "What do you see?"	"Popcorn"	Mom says, "Yes! I see the popcorn, too!"	Responsive comment
Mom says, "Say 'POPCORN'"	"Popcorn"	Mom says, "Good!"	Imitation

speech in a developmentally typical fashion (Skinner, 1957). Some children can imitate but cannot answer simple questions or use their words spontaneously, and other children can imitate and answer simple questions but not initiate.

If we view these as five separate actions, even though the form of each is the same, then we can see that we will need at least five separate lessons to assure that a child can deal with each situation appropriately. It may seem reasonable to assume that we must first teach a child to imitate before he can reply and before he can initiate communication, but in the next section, we will see that this may not be universally true.

In terms of understanding *where* we communicate, we already noted that there must be a "listener" (or someone who responds to whatever mode of communication is used) present for an episode of communication to occur. If an action, speech, or otherwise is as likely to occur when there is an audience as when a child is alone, then it is questionable whether any communication is occurring. If the child who earlier walked to the refrigerator and retrieved a can of soda (without awareness that anyone else was in the room) had been muttering "soda," would that have been a communicative act? We would say "no" because no action was directed to another person.

How Do We Communicate?

Our last investigative reporter question relates to how we communicate. The most frequent and socially accepted way to communicate is to use speech. However, when we watch someone speaking, it quickly becomes clear that we all use facial expressions and other types of body language to enhance how effective or clear our message is. I, for one, feel tortured if I am asked to speak without using my hands! We also use various voice qualities to change the way what we are saying is understood. Such changes include our tone of voice or inflection, how loudly or rapidly we speak, or how we modulate our emphasis on certain sounds, as when using sarcasm.

Of course, it is also possible to communicate without using speech and its various modifications. In the deaf community, there are several formal sign (gesture) systems, including American Sign Language (ASL) and Signing Exact English (SEE). ASL has its own set of rules for grammar, while English sign follows the rules for spoken English.

As you read this book, we are using another mode of communication, namely, writing. Although it may seem surprising, there are children who have learned to read and write but have never learned to speak. In addition to print, other symbols have been used in communication. Some written languages are picture-related, as in hieroglyphics and Chinese/Japanese, or texture-related, as in Braille. Some modern systems involve a mixture of pictures and abstract symbols, as in Blissymbols or Rebus symbols. Other communication systems involve pictures or photographs as in picture boards, the Picture Exchange Communication System, or various electronic systems. In other chapters, we will discuss how these symbols are used. The important point here is that many types of symbols have been incorporated into sophisticated communication systems.

In short, there are many modalities of communication used by children and adults (see Chapter 5 for more information on this topic). It is not necessary for a child to use speech in order to be able to communicate effectively with others. On the other hand, there *are* clear benefits if a child can use speech to communicate. These advantages include its portability (I take my voice wherever I go!), the high likelihood that it will be understood, and its ease of use.

Conclusion

Most children with autism have significant difficulties with the five W's of expressive communication discussed in this chapter. Some children with autism have far better abilities to understand others' communication than to express themselves. However, for many other children with autism, we will need to pay as close attention to teaching them to understand us as we do to teaching them to communicate. Understanding others' communication is what we describe in the next chapter.

References & Resources

Skinner, B. F. (1957). *Verbal behavior*. Englewood Cliffs, NJ: Prentice-Hall.
(A comprehensive analysis of the key functions of communication, its acquisition, and development. Best read with other professionals.)

Sulzer-Azaroff, B. & Mayer, G.R. (1991). *Behavior analysis for lasting change.* Wadsworth Publishing.
(The chapter on Communicative Behavior contains varied methods for teaching various classes of verbal or communicative behavior.)

2 | The Other Side of the Communication Coin: Understanding

Mark brought his son Richard to the school. Mark was concerned that his son had still not developed speech even though he was now three years old. Mark also was worried that his son might be deaf. I asked him why he thought this was a possibility. Mark described how his son loved to take baths and that he took one every night. He said he would call Richard's name and tell him it was time for his bath. If Richard were playing in the living room, his father would say over and over, "It's time for your bath! Let's go to your bath!" Richard would not even look up from playing with his trucks. However, if Mark turned on the faucet in the bathtub, Richard would drop everything and run to the bathroom, taking his clothes off on the fly! Mark was confused as to why Richard would not even blink when he shouted in his ears, but could hear the water being turned on upstairs in the other end of the house. Was hearing the same as understanding?

In Chapter One, we noted that communication involves at least two people. So far, we have focused our attention on the role of the person communicating with the second person. But how do we describe what the second person is doing? Usually, if I am speaking, you are listening. However, the word "listening" is not broad enough to describe everything the second person might be doing because we also pointed out that there are other modes of communication. For example, the authors are writing and you are reading. Both listen-

ing to speech and reading words involves understanding. *To help children become more skilled at communication, we need not only to improve their ability to communicate but also to improve their understanding when others communicate.*

The questions we asked about communicating *also are important to ask about* understanding communication, *often referred to as receptive language. The first question to consider is "Why understand what others communicate?"*

Why Is It Important to Understand the Communication of Others?

Just as there are two primary reasons to communicate, there are also two primary reasons to understand what someone else has communicated. For example, imagine that a girl walks into the living room and begins picking up pillows and looking under chairs as if she is searching for something. Her mother now says, "You put your candy on the TV!" The girl smiles as she walks to the TV, picks up the candy, and begins to eat. In this case, the girl listened to her mother because understanding her mother's words led her to find the candy she wanted. Therefore, sometimes we listen to what others are saying because if we understand what they say, we can get the things we like (as when we are called to dinner, to go outside to play, to see a friend, etc.).

In a different case, imagine a boy is playing in the living room. His father says, "Bring me the newspaper!" The boy stops what he is doing, finds the newspaper, and brings it to his father. His father immediately says, "Boy! What a great helper you are!" In this case, the boy listened to his father's words to get an item not for himself, but rather for his father. What the boy received was his father's praise and other social reinforcers. Therefore, sometimes we understand what others say to obtain an item we want and sometimes we understand to obtain social attention.

At times, the social attention is indirectly provided. For example, imagine a young girl who gets home from school. Her

Table 2-1 | Types of Receptive Communication

Setting	Child's Reaction	Outcome	Type of Communication
Mom says, "Bring me the popcorn"	Child gets popcorn	Mom says, "Thanks"	Follow instruction to benefit someone else
Mom says, "Eat some popcorn"	Child gets popcorn	Child eats popcorn	Follow instruction for personal gain

mother asks what happened in school that day. The girl proceeds to talk on and on about what happened with each of her friends and teachers. In this case, the girl listens to her mother's communication because it leads to additional social outcomes (that is, a longer conversation with her mother). Sometimes this type of listening occurs when there are direct questions (e.g., "What did you play with?"), while at other times we listen to indirect cues (i.e., "Boy, did I like that movie!").

When we are very young, we listen because of the immediate consequences. As we mature, we learn to listen even when the consequences are delayed. For example, we listen to what our teacher says because we know there will be test at the end of the week. We listen to the nightly news report so that we may have a more informative conversation with a friend later in the day. However, whatever the time delay to the consequence, we can still identify differences between direct versus social benefits for having listened.

What Do We Listen To?

When we are very young we learn that certain sounds are important. We hear a door opening and run to see who's there.

We hear a certain tune outside and we know the ice cream truck is on our block. We hear a dog snarl and we run the other way. We hear the water running into the tub, as in the example that begins this chapter, and know that it's bath time. Each sound becomes important because it is associated with particular events. We hear these sounds and anticipate what comes next.

However, listening to someone speak is different from hearing an important sound. The words used by people consist of particular sounds and sound combinations. Each language has its own sets of each. These sounds are combined into words and phrases and we must learn to understand what each combination means. That is, we are not born understanding the words of our own language. Fascinating to note is the experimental evidence that infants, shortly after birth, react differently to the sound of their mother's voice than they do to other sounds (including their mother's voice scrambled in novel ways). That is, even before formal language develops, children demonstrate that they know the difference between voice-related sounds and other environmental noises. Therefore, the basic "what" we listen to in a communication framework are the vocal sounds produced by other people.

When we defined functional communication in the Introduction, we noted that it is critical that children learn to approach a communicative partner. To add to that definition, it is also important that children respond to the communicative attempts of other people. A child may learn to run outside when she hears the bell of the ice cream truck, but that is a different type of learning than understanding when Mom says, "Go outside and I will buy some ice cream for you." The set of sounds in the phrase "ice cream" is important only because the group in which I communicate (i.e., those who speak English) specifically arranged for that sound set to be associated with real ice cream. If I grew up learning another language, I would not respond the same way to the sound pattern, "ice cream." The community in which a child learns a language teaches her what to listen to (rather than simply hear). For some children who have not learned to communicate or to understand, our voices are no more important than other sounds in the environment.

The "How" of Listening

When we discussed the "how" of communicating in Chapter One, we noted that there are many different modalities for successful communication. One modality involves sounds we produce when we speak. However, we also can use hand gestures and signs to effectively communicate, as well as written words, visual symbols, and various types of pictures. Furthermore, we can combine words with gestures to refine the meaning of our words.

In a similar fashion, we must learn to understand different forms of communication from other people. Not only must we learn to listen to words, but we also must learn to understand many types of visually based signals or communication. That is, we learn to understand the gestures of other people, from simple pointing to formal sign language. We learn to understand visual symbols, from traffic signs, to line drawings, to printed words. For our children to become effective at understanding communication, we must arrange for them to understand many types of visual as well as auditory modalities.

It also is important to remember that even those of us who are very competent at using speech still rely on many forms of visual systems. For example, when you come to an agreement with your employer, banker, or realtor, you don't simply trust that you (or the other person) will remember the verbal agreement—you make sure there is a written (visual) contract. That is, with your boss, you make sure that there is a visual representation of all of the critical aspects of your contract to work (i.e., how much and when you will be paid, what the benefits are, how you can renegotiate, etc.). Furthermore, most of us use some type of calendar system to help us keep track of the what, when, and where of the many things we do each week. In other words, we do not rely on our memories alone to help us recall what we are doing today, when we are supposed to go where, etc. A calendar and its entries form a visual system to help us structure the events of our lives.

When Do We Listen or Understand Others?

When are we more likely to listen to what others have to say? Generally, the greater our motivation to obtain something, the more likely we are to listen to (or watch for) communicative signs pertaining to what we want. At the end of a long school day, for instance, a student is very likely to pay close attention to the teacher's announcement that school is over so that she can go outside and play.

On the other hand, sometimes it is other people who decide that it is time to listen. For example, if a girl is playing outside the house, she may hear her mother call her name. She's likely to now run to her mother and ask, "What?" Hopefully, she will hear something important or interesting. Of course, sometimes she merely finds out that there is one more chore to do! In this case, the next time her mother calls her name, she is less likely to pay attention to what is said next.

There are a variety of phrases designed to get someone's attention, including, "Listen to me! Look at me! Come here! Stop what you're doing and listen! Pay attention!" The list is indeed long! If someone is too far away to hear your words, you may gesture for her to come closer, as when you wave your arms or motion for her to come. Only when she is close do you continue with your message.

Where Do We Listen?

While we take our ears everywhere, we don't always listen well in every setting. We learn to pay attention to what someone else is saying in certain places, but in others, we may pay little heed to what we hear. To be successful in a classroom, a student must learn to listen for the teacher's voice above all others. Yet, in the cafeteria, it becomes more important to listen to what the children around you are saying.

Some children with autism become self-focused and seem not to pay attention to what is being said to them. In quiet situations, other children with autism may readily attend to the only other person in the room. The goal is to teach the child to pay attention in other situations, even when other children and adults are present. To assist in this learning, it helps to make it more rewarding for the child to listen to us—by using powerful motivators in the group situation.

Conclusion

In this chapter, we've focused on issues related to understanding the communication of other people. Remember that a person's ability to use communication skills may be independent of the ability to understand others. Some children are able to understand what we are saying, but have great difficulty learning to speak. Other children learn to speak, but have tremendous difficulty understanding what others are saying. Some children might learn to use one modality to communicate and another one to understand others' communications. For example, one child may be able to speak but understand others best when they use visual signals. Another child may need to use visual communication strategies to communicate, but be able to understand what others are saying. Finally, while we all prefer that children learn to understand what is said to them, we also want them to learn to understand various visual signals to become effective members of our community.

References & Resources

Hodgdon, L. (1995). *Visual strategies for improving communication: Practical supports for school & home*. Troy; QuirkRoberts Pub.
(Many helpful and practical suggestions for the use of visual aides and strategies for those with various disabilities.)

3 | Can't Talk?
Can't Communicate?

I visited Doris and her three-year-old daughter, Sonja, in their home. I arrived at dinnertime and said I'd like to watch a typical meal. Doris proceeded to make dinner while Sonja banged on some pot lids. Suddenly, Sonja stood up and walked to a cabinet. She did not look at her mother, but instead started to pull on the cabinet door. The door didn't budge and Sonja started to become more and more agitated. When Doris noticed what was happening, she asked Sonja, "What do you want?" Doris opened up the door and pointed to a box of cookies and said, "This one?" Sonja continued to cry while Doris continued to hold up every box she could reach. The crying was getting louder and Doris's face was getting redder. Finally, Doris held up one box of crackers and Sonja lunged for the box. As Sonja calmed down, Doris told me how exasperated and exhausted she gets because her daughter cannot let her know which snack she wants.

Clearly, Sonja has a significant problem in expressing her needs with words. By age three to four, children typically use over 1000 words, can describe things in great detail, can discuss activities and events that are not ongoing or in their immediate surroundings, and can respond to abstract questions, such as "What color is grass?" (when there is no grass in sight). Sonja, at age three, still is not speaking or using gestures in a meaningful way.

In fact, a delay in acquiring communication skills is one of the hallmarks of autism spectrum disorders. What is the typical sequence of speech development? In general, children begin to babble around six to nine months of age. By the sixth month, children begin to demonstrate an understanding of ways to impact on their parents even without having clearly spoken words—that is, they use gestures, eye-contact, voice tone, and other body motions to influence their parents and other caregivers. Around the first birthday, most children have begun to use single words (and possibly some two-word combinations) and understand simple instructions such as, "Where's your nose?" and "Bring me your shoe." By their second birthday, most children can use approximately twenty-five to fifty words and combine them into simple sentences. They also can respond to more complex instructions, such as "Get the spoon and put it into the sink."

In contrast, the speech and communication development of children with autism and related disabilities is far less smooth. Some children are reported to engage in fairly typical babbling and early speech development but then show remarkable regression around their second birthday, often stopping to speak entirely. Other children with autism seem not to direct their speech to adults or their siblings. They may repeat things they hear on the radio, TV, or similar sources but not imitate what their parents or peers are saying. The often-meaningless repetition of words and phrases is called *echolalia,* a prominent feature for many children with autism who do develop speech. As yet, we do not fully understand the causes of these two distinct patterns of speech development. However, the result is similar—children who by the age of two or three are substantially delayed in their speech and communication development, even in comparison to the development of their other skills.

Why Do Some Children Have Difficulty Developing Speech?

One of our first questions about children who do not develop speech in the typical sequence is: Is there a single cause? The simple answer is "no." A child may fail to develop speech due to a variety of factors. Some factors are related to biological issues either present at conception or occurring during gestation. Various degrees of difficulty in developing speech are associated with mental retardation, cerebral palsy, autism, and developmental apraxia of speech (Beukelman & Mirenda, 1998). Speech impairments also may be associated with factors that are acquired after birth such as amyotrophic lateral sclerosis, multiple sclerosis (MS), traumatic brain injury, stroke, and spinal cord injury (Beukelman & Mirenda, 1998, p. 4).

In the case of autism, we do not know how the disorder is specifically related to difficulties in acquiring speech—that is, we do not yet understand what parts of the brain are influenced in such a way as to affect the development of speech. In general, there does not appear to be any distinct problem with the structural aspects of speech production (an intact tongue, lips, palate, etc.) or the motor aspects of speech production (moving the tongue, lips, jaw, etc.). Furthermore, while individual children with autism may show a history of ear infections and related temporary hearing loss, as a group such hearing difficulties do not explain the general problems in developing speech. We also do not understand why some children with autism rapidly develop speech (including speech with unusual features such as echolalia), while other children remain mute (i.e., do not use speech to effectively communicate).

Another important question is: How prevalent is the problem? This question is not easy to answer, as the definitions describing who has difficulty developing and using speech in an effective manner has varied from study to study. Recent estimates indicate that approximately 1 in 100 individuals will need significant assistance in acquiring effective communication strategies that do not depend on speech (Beukelman & Ansel, 1995).

Before relatively effective early intervention programs were designed, it was widely estimated that half of all children with autism remained mute (Silverman, 1996; Rutter, 1985). With aggressive early intervention, the rate of mutism drops substantially (to fifteen percent or less depending upon the characteristics of the children beginning the intervention). Although there are a number of programs that have reported effective interventions, such programs have in common a strong behavioral orientation, working with well-trained professionals and parents for many hours per week over two or more years (Dawson & Osterling, 1997). To learn more about such behavioral programs, a good introduction is *Right from the Start: Behavioral Intervention for Young Children with Autism,* by Sandra L. Harris and Mary Jane Weiss (Woodbine House, 1998).

What Happens If You Can't Communicate?

In our culture, the consequences for children and adults who cannot communicate are very severe. If a person cannot communicate about those things that are most important to him, then it is up to everyone else to provide the right things at the right times. Of course, even for the most caring people, many mistakes will take place.

Inability to Communicate Wants. All of us feel great frustration when we can't have the things we most want. When we feel frustrated, we end up doing things that are not pleasant to others or to ourselves. Children with significant communication deficits may display aggression, tantrums, or self-injury associated with their frustration over not being able to get what they want. (See Chapter 4.) For example, what happens if a boy wants a cookie, but his mother gives him another kind of snack because she does not know specifically what her son wants? Even though the boy may be given a snack, if it is not what he wants right now, he will feel frustrated and likely act out in some manner.

Inability to Communicate "No." How would a child react when demands keep piling up and he is not able to ask for a break? In such cases, children often strike out at others or the environment as a way of forcing escape from a difficult or unwanted task. When a child cannot politely and calmly say "No thanks!" then his physical solution will appear to be a challenging behavior management issue to others. (See Chapter 4.)

Inability to Engage in Social Conversations. What about a child who is able to communicate about fundamental needs but cannot comment or simply talk about common events across a day? Such a child may have significant difficulties in developing friendships. While we may ask our friends for special things (e.g., "Can you lend me a dollar?"), most of what happens between friends involves social interactions and consequences (e.g., "Boy, Mr. Carp is such a tough teacher!" "Wasn't that the worst movie you ever saw?" etc.). Without the ability to communicate about social events, our friendships remain limited at best.

Inability to Understand Others. What happens to children who do not understand what we are trying to communicate? For these children, the course of a day may become highly chaotic. They may not be able to understand what is going to happen next, what they are expected to do, what they will get for doing something, where they are about to go, and with whom they are about to work. Without the ability to comprehend what others are saying (or showing, in the case of visual cues), life can be bewildering and frightening.

Children who cannot understand what others are trying to communicate to them may develop complex and lengthy rituals as a way for them to make sense and establish a routine for themselves. These routines may involve self-stimulatory actions (e.g., finger flicking, rocking, etc.), routines with objects (e.g., spinning them, waving them in the air, etc.), or even verbal routines (e.g., repeating a phrase or question over and over). When such rituals are interrupted, many children become very upset and agitated. Professionals may use terms such as "resistance to change" or "maintains sameness" to describe the pattern without focusing on the cause of the pattern. (This communicative issue is just one of several factors that may contribute to the ritualistic patterns of a child.)

At a more social level, children who have trouble understanding the often-subtle social cues from their peers may appear to be awkward or socially inept. Children and adults with Asperger's syndrome generally have age-appropriate language, but display significant limitations in their ability to understand the social intricacies of society. For example, such individuals may have difficulty in understanding humor, sarcasm, and related slight modifications of phrases and words. They usually appear to be very literal. If someone were to say, "Oh, *sure!* (dripping with sarcasm) We're going outside to play," the literal child goes and puts on his coat! Tony Atwood's book (*Asperger's Syndrome: A guide for parents and teachers*, 1997) contains numerous examples of people with Asperger's syndrome and their difficulties in understanding social complexities.

The difficulty that such children have communicating effectively and understanding clearly can start a difficult downward spiral. The child may avoid trying to communicate as a result of experiencing so many failures. This withdrawal can lead to even less contact with peers. Peers in turn may think the child is more comfortable in isolation and not push for further contact. Unfortunately, if a child with autism does not interact with peers, it virtually assures that he will not develop a more mature social style, leading to further isolation. In short, it is not enough to monitor the academic progress of a child with autism—if he can't use his skills interacting with other people, he will not become successful in the adult world.

Who Can Benefit from Acquiring Non-speech Communication Skills?

The short answer is that an alternate method of communication should be considered for any child (generally, eighteen months of age or older) who cannot:

- use words or approximations to request favorite items;
- use words or approximations to comment about interesting things;
- initiate, imitate, and respond to simple questions;

- understand much of what others say, especially about retrieving simple items, following simple instructions, and responding to social signals.

These are skills that are learned by typically developing children by the time they are about two years old.

If a child cannot accomplish these communicative functions via speech, then we must consider using an alternative or augmentative communication system (AAC). In general, *alternative* is used to refer to methods of communication that replace speech, such as sign language or picture-based systems. *Augmentative* refers to enhancements of a child's current communication skills, such as by using visual signals to help remind him about the choices there are available in a particular situation or pictures to enhance speech that is difficult to understand. AAC systems involve either the use of gestures and sign language or depend on various visual symbols, including pictures, photographs, icons, and/or words. See Chapter 5 for an overview of types of AAC.

The following are some guidelines to help you determine whether AAC could benefit your child. Parents will find it helpful to have professionals assist in collecting the necessary information and making a deliberate choice

1. How old is the child?

Children younger than eighteen months who do not effectively produce vocalizations or imitate speech may not raise professional concerns about their development. These children may show typical skills in following directions and in playing with adults and peers. They may be simply slow to develop speech while other forms of communication, including gestures, may be developing appropriately.

However, if children younger than two years are not only slow to develop speech but are also lagging in the development of social responsiveness (i.e., responding when others smile, speak, or attempt to play), as well as in imitation and play, then significant concerns about development are appropriate. If your child is in this category, it is critically important to obtain a professional assessment from a psychologist or developmental specialist, as well as a speech-language pathologist capable of completing an audiology screening.

At the other end of the time scale, there is considerable evidence that children older than seven years are unlikely to develop independent speech if they haven't already done so. To be sure, there are sporadic testimonials about speech acquisition in older children, but these appear to be rare. For older children who do not communicate through speech, focusing on the acquisition of functional communication skills via alternative modalities would be most appropriate.

2. How long has the child received quality training in vocal imitation?

When children are two years or older and do not speak, many professionals (including speech-language pathologists and behavior analysts) have promoted the development of speech via vocal imitation training (e.g., Lovaas, 1981; Lovaas, 1987). Vocal imitation training teaches a child to repeat simple sounds (usually ones he can already make) and then moves on to imitation of sound combinations, simple words, and eventually simple phrases.

The success rate for vocal imitation programs has been very encouraging. However, there are a fair number of students who do not become good vocal imitators within three months of intense training. The estimates on this pool of children range from ten to thirty percent. When vocal imitation training has been tried for three or more months without success, focus should be placed on teaching functional communication skills via another modality (see Lovaas, 1987). This is not to suggest that vocal imitation training should cease. From our perspective, training should focus on functional communication skills (such as those described in subsequent chapters) that will be rapidly effective, and vocal imitation should continue to be addressed. For many children, these two areas—functional communication and vocalization—

may merge at some time in the future. (See Chapter 6 for examples of this type of outcome.)

3. How does the child currently use his vocalizations?

As Chapter One discusses, a child uses a particular word for one of two reasons (requesting or commenting). He can also use it for either of these purposes in different situations (i.e., initiate vs. imitate vs. respond to questions). If your child can only *imitate* single words, he may not be able to use spoken words for functional communication. If so, you should consider either: a) rapidly promoting non-imitative uses of spoken words, or b) introducing a modality that promotes functional communication while addressing expansion of imitation and other aspects of vocalization.

For example, a two-year-old girl may be able to imitate ten words. She may even be able to sing a few simple jingles she has heard on the television. However, when offered a favorite snack or toy, she remains silent unless someone models the exact word for the desired item. In this case, the girl is not initiating with the few spoken words she is able to produce. Although we would want to continue to expand this child's imitative skills, we should also address her immediate need to initiate functional communication.

In the next chapter, we will provide some information to help you understand what your child could be communicating with his behavior if he does not yet have another way of communicating. The following chapters will discuss different nonverbal communication methods that could benefit your child.

References & Resources

Atwood, T. (1997). *Asperger's Syndrome: A guide for parents and teachers.* Jessica Kingsley Publishers.

Beukelman, D. & Ansel, B. (1995). Research priorities in augmentative and alternative communication. *Augmentative and Alternative Communication, 11,* 131-134.

Beukelman, D. & Mirenda, P. (1998). *Augmentative and alternative communication: Management of severe communication disorders in children and adults (2nd ed)*. Baltimore: Paul H. Brookes.

Dawson, G. & Osterling, J. (1997). Early intervention in autism. In M.J. Guralnick (Ed.), *The effectiveness of early intervention* (pp. 307-326). Baltimore: Paul H. Brookes.

Harris, S. & Weiss, M.J. (1998). *Right from the start: Behavioral intervention for young children with autism*. Bethesda: Woodbine House.

Lovaas, O.I. (1981). *Teaching developmentally disabled children: The me book*. Austin, TX: PRO-ED.

Lovaas, O.I. (1987). Behavioral treatment and normal educational and intellectual functioning in young autistic children. *Journal of Consulting and Clinical Psychology, 55,* 3-9.

Reichle, J., York, J., & Sigafoos, J. (1991). *Implementing augmentative and alternative communication: Strategies for learners with severe disabilities*. Baltimore: Paul H. Brookes.
(An excellent resource for strategies with children and adults with complex communication difficulties—designed for a professional audience.)

Rutter, M. (1985). The treatment of autistic children. *Journal of Child Psychology & Psychiatry, 26,* 193-214.

Silverman, F. (1995). *Communication for the speechless (3rd ed.)*. Boston: Allyn & Bacon.

4 | Why Is She Doing That? The Relationship between Behavior and Communication

At a parent meeting, Susan described her current problems with her son, Nathan. She knew that he enjoyed playing in the backyard. Her problem was knowing exactly when he wanted to go outside. She told the group that sometimes Nathan would stand by the back door and start to scream. If no one came quickly, he would flop down and start to bang his head on the floor. Once that happened, Susan believed that the only thing that would calm him down was to open the door and let him go outside. Once outside, he quickly stopped crying, and Susan could go back to whatever she was doing.

As we saw in Chapter One, some behaviors are communicative, while others are not. We should add that some of the communicative actions of children, especially those with disabilities, often are not exactly what we adults would like to see! For example, Nathan's way of communicating that he wanted to go outside was not a form his parents enjoyed.

A child's behavioral difficulties, including tantrums and aggression, often remain first and foremost in our minds. At the end of a long school day, we teachers are far more likely to talk to our partners about the trouble we had today (e.g., "She hit me again") than the positive things that occurred (e.g., "She smiled three times today"). Therefore, the tendency of teachers and parents is to try to eliminate these problems immediately.

However, the best solutions come about by determining why the child is behaving as she is and then replacing that behavior with one that is more acceptable to us and accomplishes her goals. Therefore, in this chapter we will look into the relationship between different types of behavioral problems and their link to communicative alternatives.

Behavior Management Problems That Act as Communication

Actions of children that we adults would like to see disappear are sometimes referred to by behavior analysts as "behavior management targets." These targets may serve particular needs of children, such as helping the child gain access to concrete outcomes. For example, acting a certain way may result in going outside to play, getting cookies at the check-out counter in the supermarket, getting food that someone else is eating, etc.

On the other hand, some targets result in increased attention from other people. For example, what would you do if you walked into a room and saw a very young child screaming and slapping her face? I know that my tendency would be to pick up the child to soothe her as quickly as possible and then to try to find out what was wrong. However, what if the child had no systematic effective communication system? In that case, she would not be able to communicate about the problem. Still, she may have enjoyed being picked up. What will happen the next time that she sees me? If I do not quickly pick her up, she is very likely to start crying and slapping her face. From her point of view, that is what "worked" last time—crying and slapping seemed to result in my picking her up.

In such cases, the child's actions depend on my presence and serve a communicative function—requesting a desired outcome. It is important to note that we can identify a communicative function only if the child primarily engages in the action when someone else is present. If the child engages in the action when we are present as often as when we are absent, then we could not say that the child's action was directed toward a potential communicative partner. As discussed earlier, the essence of communication involves behavior directed toward another person.

Other actions of children and adults may serve a different communicative function—namely, escape or avoidance. For example, when given a difficult task, a child may begin to scream and hit herself.

I met Ruth while visiting a school for teenagers with severe cognitive limitations. At the time, Ruth was sixteen years old and had no speech or other formal communication system. I had been asked to observe her because she was reported to have become increasingly aggressive and self-injurious. I observed her sitting in her classroom. A teacher approached and said, "Ruth, it's time to work." The teacher showed Ruth a box filled with vocational materials. Ruth immediately began screaming while forcefully punching her thighs with her fist and biting the back of her other hand. The teacher calmly walked away with the box. Twenty minutes later, the teacher returned with another box of materials and the same message. Again, Ruth screamed and hurt herself. The teacher removed herself and the materials. After another twenty minutes, the teacher returned, issued her direction, and showed Ruth a box containing a comb and brush. Ruth calmly took the comb and brush and started brushing her hair. Ruth was a very effective communicator!

In trying to understand Ruth's actions, several factors are important to consider. First, when Ruth was left alone, she sat quietly and did not engage in screaming or self-injury. Next, she did not begin the tantrum until she looked at the materials that her teacher offered. If she liked the materials and associated activity (i.e., the hairbrush) she calmly proceeded with the activity. If she did not like what she saw, then she screamed and hit herself (and the teacher if she approached). The teacher then removed the materials and Ruth gradually calmed down. Her action was communicative because it occurred when the teacher approached and it was an effective way to get her teacher to remove the unwanted items. That is, Ruth was able to avoid working on activities she didn't like because her teacher would remove things after Ruth started the tantrum. If Ruth had had formal functional communication skills, she would have been able to communicate that she did not want to do certain tasks (e.g., "I don't like that job"; "No thanks!" etc.). Then her teacher could have discussed why it was an important activity or offered a better incentive for Ruth.

In addition to learning how to use their behavior to avoid certain activities, many children and adults learn how to escape from some activities. These activities may be:

1. difficult,
2. boring,
3. too long in duration,
4. associated with too little positive feedback (as in, "Hey, the pay around here is terrible!"),
5. in environments that are too noisy, crowded, chaotic, cold/hot, etc.

As an adult, it is likely that you have had to work (or study) in situations or environments in which one of these factors was in effect. Most adults, however, have learned communicative skills that may help in such circumstances. Instead of simply screaming and running away (which we have all considered!), we may ask for a break—some time away from the job. We could also communicate about issues that may help improve the work situation—such as asking for help, asking for more supervision, increasing the number of scheduled breaks each day, opening a window, etc.

Behavior Management Problems That Are Not Communicative

So far, we have reviewed that certain behaviors may serve a communicative function related to:

1. obtaining a reinforcing outcome,
2. escaping from a person, item, or activity, or
3. avoiding an item, person, or activity.

However, not every behavior management target serves one of these communicative functions. Remember, as Chapter One discusses, not all behaviors are communicative. Sometimes, we simply act on the world without any communicative involvement of another person. Furthermore, sometimes we do things that are not viewed as purposeful or rational. That is, some of our actions are best viewed as reactions to the circumstances at hand.

One day, I (AB) walked into a large office building intending to visit the state office on the thirty-fifth floor. I had visited this office many times over the past few years. As in the past and without anyone in sight, I calmly pushed the elevator button. On this day, however, nothing happened. I stood for a moment and noticed that the elevator had not arrived. I pushed the button again. Still no response. Now I pushed the button in several quick, hard bursts. Still nothing happened. I began pounding on the button with great effort. I also noticed, without a sense of pride, that I was muttering a series of unspeakable curses. Suddenly, my boss approached. I stopped cursing and pounding and calmly said that the elevator seemed to be out of service.

We imagine that each of you has had a similar experience. Obviously, this type of behavior is *not* communicative. Although I did say a few choice words, they were not meant to be heard by anyone else, as demonstrated by my change in behavior when I saw my boss. This behavior was also not rational and learned from experience. Not only does this pounding on the button rarely work, this type of reaction occurs the first time we encounter a recalcitrant piece of machinery. Furthermore, I don't recall any lessons from my mother in which she said, "Now, here is what to do if the elevator gets stuck...." The question remains, why do we do this type of explosive reaction?

For me, getting to the thirty-fifth floor was important because it was the only way to get to my job, which meant it was the way to get my pay (no work, no pay). When you and I, and our children, encounter situations in which we expect to get a rewarding outcome, and that outcome is delayed or removed, we react in this emotional manner.

One other circumstance that may elicit similar emotional reactions is being in pain. Studies with laboratory animals have indicted that if an animal is paired with another animal and is given unavoidable pain (via electric shock), then the animal that is shocked is very likely to become aggressive to its companion. This aggression does not help reduce the rate of the shock but it is still a reliable outcome to this circumstance. Other research has indicated that if an animal is alone, and receives unavoidable shock, it may begin to injure itself. For obvious reasons, such work has not been done on children (with or without disabilities). However, Ray Romanczyk (Romanczyk & Matthews, 1998) has collected data regarding some children who forcefully hit their own heads, demonstrating that when they were in pain (as measured by pressure on their eardrum during an infection) they were much more likely to hit themselves than when they were not in pain.

In short, there can be many possible explanations for any given behavior we observe. Some may involve communication, such as when a girl hits her head, indicating that she wants attention, to leave the area, or that she dislikes something being presented to her. However, that same behavior may also occur without involving communication, such as reacting to the loss of an expected reward, or to pain. How we explain the head-hitting will influence the type of intervention we design for the girl. If we decide her actions are communicative, we can use some of the techniques described in Chapters five, six, and seven to teach her a better way to communicate. If we decide her actions are noncommunicative, we can use strategies in Chapter eight to help her better handle her frustrations.

What Is Functional Communication Training?

One reason we emphasize the *why* associated with a behavior and not just its form (the *how*) is because we assume that there are several ways to achieve the same goal. That is, if a child is trying to gain attention, then we will assume that there are many different actions that she could use to achieve the same outcome—gaining attention. If this is a safe assumption, then our plan may be to teach the child another way to gain attention—one that does not involve self-injury or other disruptive actions.

An area of study, termed *functional communication training (FCT),* is devoted to investigating this general strategy of determining the reasons underlying behavior and then teaching different ways to achieve the desired outcome. In one of the first studies of FCT (Carr and Durand, 1985), two researchers worked with children displaying aggression or self-injury. They found two distinct reasons for these behavior management concerns. Some children appeared to act out when they were given work that was very difficult. Their problematic behaviors appeared to communicate their need for help. A second set of children appeared to become upset if the teacher was not paying them attention, whether the lesson was easy or difficult. Their problematic behaviors appeared to communicate their need for encouraging feedback from the teacher. The question was, what should each group of children be taught?

The children who appeared to need help were taught to request help using a simple phrase. Once they were able to communicate this request, help was provided. After learning this skill, these children showed clear improvements in their difficult behaviors. The other children were taught to say, "How am I doing?" When staff heard this question, they immediately praised the child for working on the lesson. Again, once this skill was learned, significant improvements were noticed. What is equally interesting is that these researchers studied what would happen if a child were taught the skill that did not fit his or her problem.

That is, children who needed help with a difficult task were taught to say, "How am I doing?" Staff would respond to this statement but not the child's need for help (since the child did not ask for help). Learning statements that did not result in the needed outcome did not help the children behave more appropriately.

Therefore, if we are to teach a new communication skill to replace a problematic behavior that a child uses as a communication strategy, then we must be certain that the new skill accomplishes exactly what the child was trying to accomplish. That is, children who need help must be taught to ask for help, while those needing more feedback need to learn to request feedback. Similarly, children who need to take a break from a boring or difficult activity must learn to request a break. The function of the new skill must match the function of the old behavior management target. Research has suggested that it should not take any more effort to use the new skill than it does to perform the action being replaced (Frea & Vittemberg, 2000).

How Do We Determine the Functional Control of a Behavior?

There are several strategies to help us figure out why someone is engaging in a particular behavior. (This is referred to as the *functional control* of the behavior by behavior analysts.) In general, the idea is to identify the *antecedents* of the behavior (i.e., what occurs before it), as well as the *consequences* (i.e., what the child gets out of the behavior).

A functional *assessment* can be conducted by interviewing teachers, parents, and other helpers in a systematic fashion using a structured checklist (Charlop-Christy & Kelso, 1997). A more intense form of assessment can be conducted by carefully collecting data regarding the relationship between the behavior and various factors, including

    a. time of day,

    b. activity,

    c. people present,

  d. length of activity,

  e. presence of demands (including a high rate of instructions, new instructions, etc.),

  f. removing or denying access to reinforcing items.

  Knowledgeable staff can add other factors. Once sufficient occurrences of the problem behavior have been observed, it is possible to correlate the potential factors with the likelihood of the behavior occurring. While such correlations do not prove the relationship, they can help point out factors that are most likely to be contributing to your child's problem behavior.

  The most precise information on the causes of behavior can be collected via a formal *functional analysis.* In this type of study, staff trained in behavior analysis make specific environmental modifications (e.g., adding demands, ignoring the behavior, providing a stimulating environment vs. a boring environment) and then monitor corresponding changes in the child's target behavior. While this procedure yields the most accurate information about the potential causes of the behavior in question, it also is quite demanding.

  Under the Individuals with Disabilities Education Act (IDEA) your child's school must agree to conduct a functional behavior analysis if: 1) she has behaviors that are interfering with her learning at school, and 2) if she is receiving special education services. Parents can arrange for a behavior analyst to conduct this assessment, but a school team can choose to develop a plan independent of recommendations from the parent's consultant.

When Is the Best Time to Teach Alternative Communication Skills?

  After you have recognized that your child is having a behavior problem due to difficulty communicating, and have figured out what her behavior is meant to communicate, you need to look for opportunities to teach her an alternate way to communicate her message. As the story below illustrates, not every moment is a "teaching moment" for children with autism.

I watched Gina playing with several toys. She picked up one piece and tried to fit it into another piece. She pushed and pushed but the parts would not fit. She began to rock, then whimper, and then scream. She threw down the piece and then scattered every piece within reach. She was now in the midst of a full-blown tantrum! I walked over to Gina and calmly said, "You need to ask for help!" Gina whimpered, "Help!" I guided her to connect the pieces and she continued to play quietly. However, I reminded myself that Gina and I had gone through this same sequence yesterday, and the day before that, and the day before that, and ....

Early in my career (*AB*), I used this strategy and watched many other people using similar tactics. We would observe a child's problem and then encourage her to "use her language" to solve the problem. However, I found that if I used this strategy, the child continued to have tantrums in difficult situations, and only asked for help when I reminded her. It took me many years to figure out that the child had learned precisely what I had taught. From her perspective: a) If you have a broken toy, start screaming, then ... b) Andy will come over and tell you to say something, then ... c) Say what Andy wants and he will help you!

The reason that Gina was not learning to request help was that I was not teaching her to recognize the situation as one in which she should spontaneously request help. I had taught her that I would recognize that she needed help (by watching her have a tantrum) and then would remind her to use her words. I realized that if I wanted to teach Gina to ask for help, I must teach her to ask for help before she has the tantrum. That is, if I am watching Gina having a tantrum, I must prepare to start a lesson after the tantrum has ended.

In general, teaching any new skill in the midst of a tantrum or other type of emotional display is very difficult. A better long-term solution is to re-create the problem situation and guide the child through an effective alternative. In this way, we are striving to prevent tantrums from starting rather than emphasizing how to eliminate them once begun. Just as it took Andy years to learn how to effectively teach this lesson, most children require many opportunities to acquire a skill. A teacher must have patience to know that there will be more opportunities in the future, and need not teach a lesson that will make the child more dependent. Teachers must create situations in which the child becomes more independent in her use of spontaneous communication.

In our example with Gina, a more effective strategy would be to first give her a toy that didn't work as she expected. As soon as she noticed the problem, and before she started the tantrum, she would be helped to communicate, "Help!" (See the next page for step-by-step instructions.)

Conclusion

In this chapter, we've reviewed many types of behavioral difficulties your child may display. The best solutions will involve:

1. Determine what is causing the behavior.
2. If the behavior is communicative, what is your child trying to communicate?
3. Determine a good alternative communicative behavior.
4. Determine whether your child can already use this alternative. If not, teach the new communicative alternative behavior.
5. Create many opportunities for your child to use this new alternative.

In our next chapter we will review several communication options for children who are not using speech. After that, we will focus on using one of those methods (PECS) with children with autism.

How to Begin Teaching a Child to Communicate "Help!"

Materials needed:
A favorite toy that you have sabotaged so that it doesn't work.

Teachers needed:
One teacher to create the problem situation;
Another teacher to manually assist the child

Background:
Harry, who does not speak and is just learning to communicate, likes to play with a motorized firetruck that has a flashing light and a siren. His mother, Lily, has observed that if the firetruck isn't working properly (i.e., the battery has run down, the wheels get stuck, the siren doesn't sound, etc.) then Harry throws down the truck, screams, and starts to fiercely slap his head. When Lily has seen this happen, she has quickly fixed the truck to stop Harry from hurting himself.

Teaching scenario:
Lily has asked her daughter, Doris, to help teach Harry to calmly request help. Lily asks Doris to sit behind him. Without Harry seeing her, Lily takes the battery out of the firetruck and then hands the truck to Harry. He quickly takes it and turns on the switch to make the siren sound and the lights flash. Nothing happens! At the earliest signs of agitation, Doris quickly helps Harry pick up the truck and give it to Lily. Lily immediately says, "Oh, you need help!" while giving Harry the battery and helping him put it into the truck. Harry then tries the switch again and is very happy that the truck now works. During the next few days, Lily and Doris repeat this lesson with Doris gradually reducing her assistance. By the end of the week, when the truck doesn't work, Harry picks up

the truck on his own and gives it to his mother. His mother and Doris switch roles so that Harry quickly learns to ask for help from whomever is nearby. Over time, his mother creates new problems for Harry to solve with his new skill, including a container that won't open, a juice box without a straw in it, and a small radio that isn't working.

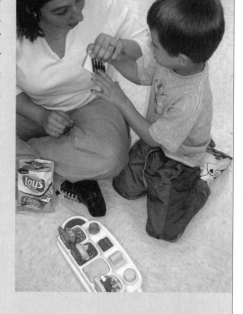

Long-term strategies:

This initial strategy—giving your child things that don't work right—is similar to what everyone observes typically developing children do at a very young age. Just as these children learn to refine their ability to ask for help over time, so, too, will Harry learn to adjust his skills. For example, he may learn to use a "help" symbol within a visual communication system. The strategies to teach him how to use such a symbol will be the same as described in Chapter 6. The benefit of using two teachers for the initial aspects of this lesson will hold true whether Harry uses visual symbols, sign (formal or informal), or speech.

References & Resources

Carr, E. G. & Durand, V. M. (1985). Reducing behavior problems through functional communication training. *Journal of Applied Behavior Analysis, 18,* 111-126.

Charlop-Christy, M.H. & Kelso, S.E. (1997). *How to treat the child with autism* (Chapter 1). Claremont, CA: Claremont McKenna College.

Frea, W.D. & Vittemberg, G.L (2000). Behavioral interventions for children with autism. In J. Austin & J.E. Carr (Eds), *Handbook of applied behavior analysis.* (pp. 247-273). Reno, NV: Context Press.

Koegel, R. & Koegel, L. (1996). *Teaching children with autism: strategies for initiating positive interactions and improving learning opportunities.* Baltimore: Paul H. Brookes.
(A reader-friendly book describing many ways to promote the development of many useful skills with children with autism.)

Romanczyk, R.G. & Matthews, A. (1998). Physiological state as antecedent: utilization in functional analysis. In J.K. Luiselli & M.J. Cameron (Eds.), *Antecedent control procedures for the behavioral support of persons with developmental disabilities.* Baltimore: Paul H. Brookes.

5 | Augmentative and Alternative Communication Systems

by Pat Mirenda, Ph.D.

Pamela is a ten-year-old girl who has autism and limited speech. Despite this, she is a successful communicator both at school and at home. When she wants something within her visual range, she leads a family member, classmate, or teacher to it and vocalizes. When she wants something that is out of sight or in another location, she points to line drawing symbols in a communication book. Pamela also uses line drawing symbols for her daily schedule and as a component of her reading curriculum. During recess and lunchtime, she and her friends enjoy looking through her communication book, in which there are pictures of Pam, her family, and her friends doing fun activities (like trick or treating on Halloween!).

During writing or math activities in her classroom, Pamela uses a computer to write, because she has difficulty manipulating a pencil and paper. She also uses a computer at home to play games with her sister and her dad. Last but certainly not least, Pam uses her limited speech to greet people, ask for help, and say "no!" when she doesn't like what is happening.

Pamela is a very fortunate child! It is clear that she has been supported by family members and school personnel who understand that her lack of speech doesn't mean she has nothing to say, and who have made systematic efforts to provide her with an individualized augmentative and alternative communication (AAC) system. Just like you and I do, Pamela communicates in a variety of ways, depending on the situation. One AAC technique will *never* meet all of a child's communication needs, so a combination of approaches will be needed. This is important to remember when supporting children with autism who are just beginning to learn about communication. In this chapter, the combination of all of the symbols and devices used by a child is referred to as his or her AAC *system*.

What Is AAC?

The term augmentative and alternative communication (AAC) refers to interventions designed to compensate for the expressive communication impairments of individuals. The word *augmentative* suggests that these interventions can be used to improve upon the effectiveness of communication through existing means (including speech), while *alternative* implies developing systems that temporarily or permanently replace speech.

A host of modalities can be used to augment or replace speech, including:

- residual speech,
- vocalizations,
- pictures or related visual symbols (from photographs to print),
- Braille,
- gestures (informal or within a formal system such as American Sign Language), or
- various switch-activated devices (operated by any body action, including eye gaze).

Each of these modalities is explored in detail below.

Under the Individuals with Disabilities Education Act (IDEA), AAC systems are considered a type of "assistive technology." The recent (1997) amendment to IDEA assures the right of every child to have an assessment regarding the need for assistive technology. When children are determined to need assistive technology, including AAC, the public school has an obligation to provide the necessary devices or adaptations (and the training to support staff in its use) at no cost to the child's family. Parents or teachers who believe a child may need such assistance should insist on adding an AAC specialist as a consult to the child's educational team.

For more information about the field of AAC in general, the International Society for Augmentative and Alternative Communication (ISAAC) has provided useful information to professionals and lay people for almost twenty years. (See the Resource Guide at the end of the book.)

Why Use AAC?

AAC techniques can reduce the frustration experienced by many children with autism who do not speak. As you read in Chapter 3, teaching communication alternatives is one way to reduce or prevent behavior problems that stem from frustration. For example, AAC techniques can be used to teach children to ask for what they want, ask for help, or ask for a break from an activity instead of tantruming, screaming, or engaging in other problem behaviors. Children can be taught to use manual signs, photographs, line drawings, or other symbols for this purpose. When a child learns to communicate via any modality, he then will be able to better participate in play and other school activities, and is more likely to be perceived in a more positive light by peers.

What about Speech Development?

One of the most common concerns expressed by parents and teachers regarding the use of AAC techniques with children with autism is how it is likely to affect speech development. The good news is that there is ample evidence that AAC techniques do *not* interfere with the development of speech—in fact, AAC may *promote* speech development in some children. For example, in Chapter 6 you will read about the Picture Exchange Communication

System (PECS), an instructional approach for teaching children how to use symbols to communicate. You will also read about some of the outcome data from PECS that suggests that many children who initially learn to communicate in this way develop speech over time. It appears that once children have learned to use between 30-100 symbols to communicate using PECS, they often begin to speak. Many are eventually able to use only speech for communication and discontinue the use of PECS altogether.

Additional support for speech development with AAC use was provided through a research project conducted with thirteen children and adolescents with severe disabilities, two of whom had autism. All of the participants had ten or fewer spoken word approximations at the start of the project. They were provided with an AAC intervention called the System for Augmenting Language (SAL) over a two-year period (Romski & Sevcik, 1996). Communication displays using symbols accompanied by printed words were constructed for each participant. The displays were placed on small computerized communication devices that produced synthetic speech when the symbols were touch-activated. (For example, if the symbol for "juice" was activated, the device said "juice.") Communication partners were taught to activate the symbols on the devices as they spoke to the children in naturally occurring communication interactions. For example, a parent might say to a child, "Johnny, let's go outside and play," while activating the symbols for "outside" and "play" on his device. The children were encouraged, though not required, to use their devices throughout the day.

Seven of the thirteen participants, including the two with autism, increased their proportions of intelligible spoken words over the course of the project. The researchers speculated that the consistent models of spoken words provided by the devices immediately following each symbol usage might have contributed to the children's speech development.

There is also evidence that using sign language as an AAC system does not interfere with the development of speech. One study found that when children with autism can use 200 or more signs and can use combinations of signs, many acquire functional speech (Layton & Watson, 1995).

In short, there is no evidence that using AAC will interfere with or inhibit the development of speech and there is growing evidence suggesting a positive impact on speech acquisition.

Types of AAC Symbols

Communicating without speech requires the use of alternative symbols. A symbol is something that stands for something else. There are two main types of AAC symbols: unaided and aided. Unaided symbols do not require any equipment to produce, and include gestures, body language, vocalizations, and manual signs (among others). Aided symbols require devices that are external to the individuals who use them, such as communication books, voice output communication devices, and computers. In the next section, we will review the most commonly used AAC symbols (both unaided and aided) and discuss some of the primary advantages and disadvantages of each.

Unaided Symbols

Natural Gestures and Body Language

Before children learn to use speech, they engage in a wide array of communicative gestures. Some of these gestures appear to be natural extensions of other actions. For example, pointing is very similar in form to reaching for something. Others seem to develop as an extension or a pantomime of actions. For example, if a basketball player is about to shoot a foul shot in a basketball game and sees an opponent holding his hands around his own neck, he may tell himself not to "choke." Still other gestures are more formal, and, like spoken words, have meanings only within a given culture. For example, in North America, most people know that the "V" sign made with the fingers means either "victory" or "peace" (depending on the age of the person making the gesture).

Although many gestures involve hand motions, we also use other parts of our bodies to convey messages. I can shrug my shoulders in doubt, frown in puzzlement, or hold out my hands and arms to ask for assistance. Perhaps the most familiar gesture involves nodding and shaking the head to mean "yes" or "no."

People use gestures to communicate many types of messages. Perhaps the most obvious is communication about wants and needs. For example, we may hold out two toys to a child, ask, "Which one do you want to play with?" and expect the child to point to or simply take the desired toy. Similarly, before they are two years old, typical children learn that they can get help from adults by simply bringing objects to them. They also learn that they can get people to look at objects or events of interest by pointing to them. Other gestures, such as waving hi or bye, blowing a kiss, and playing peek-a-boo, are used for purely social reasons. Still, they are extremely important in developing smooth social interactions between friends or between children and adults.

Why are gestures important? A common mistake in teaching communication skills to children with autism is neglecting the importance of natural gestures as components of a communication system. This mistake often occurs because many parents and teachers tend to view communication as an "either-or" skill: either the child communicates this way *or* the child communicates that way—which, of course, is not the case! Because children with autism have so much difficulty learning what communication is all about, it is important to respond to and encourage them to use *all* forms of communication, as long as those forms are understandable and socially acceptable. For example, when Joshua leads his father to the cupboard to ask for a treat, or when Juanita cries after she falls down and skins her knee, they are communicating messages ("I want something" and "Ow! That hurt!") that should be respected and acknowledged.

How can gestural use be encouraged? Children with autism are likely to benefit from playful interactions that encourage them to use gestures to communicate. An example is the "Row, row, row your boat" game that Joshua's dad plays with him every evening before bedtime. Josh and his father sit on the floor facing each other with their feet touching, and they hold hands. While Josh's dad chants the "Row, row, row your boat" song, they rock back and forth to the tune. Every few lines, Josh's dad pauses in the song and waits for Josh to pull on his hands or make a noise before he continues. When they first started playing this game, Josh didn't know what to do, and would often just sit there when his dad paused. But little by little, Josh started to use body language and vocalizations during the pauses, and his dad responded right away by continuing the game. By responding to Josh's behaviors, his dad did a great job of teaching Josh to ask for "more!" Soon, Josh began to pull on people's hands and to vocalize in other situations as well, when he wanted "more."

This playful orientation can be adapted to other situations. For example, if your child likes to be picked up and spun around, you could first spin him around, then put him down and wait for him to raise his hands to indicate he wants to be picked up again. Initially, you might have to raise his arms for him, saying something like, "You want to go up again?" Little by little, you would withdraw your physical assistance until he was reaching his arms up to you himself. These examples show how easy it is to practice using gestures in the context of playful interactions and routines.

How can gestures be taught directly? It is likely that typical children learn to use gestures for communication by imitating the gestures made by adults and other children. Most children with autism have difficulty learning to communicate through gestures, at least in part because of their known difficulty with imitation (Stone, Ousley, & Littleford, 1997; Stone, Ousley, Yoder, Hogan, & Hepburn, 1997). Thus, how we teach a child with autism to use gestures directly will largely depend on other skills the child displays.

If your child *can* imitate head and hand actions, then demonstrating various gestures and their meanings will be quite helpful in teaching. On the other hand, if he *cannot* imitate, demonstrating gestures is likely to be unsuccessful. In such cases, teaching him to imitate will be important for the acquisition of many skills, including the use of gestures. However, while you teach imitation, you can also help your child acquire useful gestures by physically assisting him to make the motions required.

The key to using physical assistance to teach gestures is creating situations in which the gestures will prove important to your child. If gestures are not taught within situations where they are typically used and truly important, it is unlikely your child will learn to use them spontaneously. For example, consider the gesture of "waving hello." It is clear that there are several types of situations in which this is an appropriate action. If Dad enters a room and waves hello to Mark, then it would be appropriate for Mark to wave back. In addition, when Mark walks into a room, even if Dad doesn't wave hello, it would be appropriate for Mark to initiate and wave hello to him. Such natural situations would be excellent times for someone who acts as the "teacher" (such as Mom or another adult) to physically prompt Mark to wave "hello."

Physical prompts may start out fully hand-over-hand, but may be *faded* (i.e., reduced in strength) gradually in intensity and type over a series of opportunities. In general, the more important the outcome is to your child, the more likely it is that he will tolerate physical prompting. Over time, the positive and enthusiastic reaction he gets from dad is likely to result in him learning to use this gesture as a greeting.

For additional information on teaching children with autism to imitate social gestures, you may want to read *Reaching Out, Joining In: Teaching Social Skills to Young Children with Autism* by Mary Jane Weiss and Sandra L. Harris (Woodbine House, 2001).

What about teaching children to understand gestures? It is important to teach children to understand gestures as well as to use them. Otherwise, it is difficult to communicate messages efficiently and rapidly in many situations. For example, one important gesture for a child to understand is what we mean when we point to something. Usually, we at least want the child to look at what we are pointing to. Sometimes, we also want the child to retrieve an item that is pointed out ("Get that"), to put something in the direction we point ("Put it there"), or to remain in the place we point to ("Wait right here"). We usually accompany pointing with verbal directions to clarify the exact message—but the pointing itself is a critical part of the interaction. Similarly, gestures that involve social routines, such as waving goodbye, giving a "high five," or clapping to show approval, are important for the child to understand if communication is to be effective and efficient.

To teach your child to understand gestures, you first must be certain that the gesture you are teaching is truly important to him. For example, let's go back to the "pointing" example and consider Harry's situation. Harry likes to complete puzzles and thus enjoys getting each puzzle piece to complete the task. His mom decides to put all of the puzzle pieces in a box except for the first few, to provide a motivating context for teaching Harry to understand what she means when she points. When Harry begins to look for the next puzzle piece, she points to the box and then immediately taps it with her finger. Harry looks at the box when he hears the tap, lifts the lid, and takes a puzzle piece. Over the next several trials, instead of immediately tapping after pointing, mom gradually increases the delay between the two actions. Over time, Harry learns to respond to mom's point as a signal to get the next piece. This time-delay technique can be adapted to teach children to understand other types of gestures as well. (See Heckaman, Alber, Hooper, & Heward, 1998 for more information about this procedure).

Manual Signs

You are probably familiar with the language systems of manual signs used by people who are deaf. Some individuals who are able to hear but have difficulty understanding and/or producing speech—such as children with autism—may also use manual signs. There are several different systems in which people use movements by their fingers and hands (augmented by other body actions) that represent letters, words, or phrases.

Manual signs can be used for both expressing and understanding language. Manual sign *input* (understanding) occurs when people who communicate to the child use signs to augment their speech. For example, Felicia's teacher speaks at the same time she signs the key words in her message. So, when it is time to do math, she tells Felicia to "Get out your book and a pencil" while signing *get, book,* and *pencil*. She does this because Felicia seems to pay attention more readily and follow directions more accurately if she is provided with signed information in addition to speech. To be sure, some children only *seem* to listen better when sign is added to speech, when in fact they are only relying on the visual cues. For each child, it is important to try to determine whether combining modes of input actually helps.

Manual sign *output* (expression) occurs when the child with autism uses manual signs to communicate to others. For example, when Matt wants to use the family computer at home, he asks his mom to turn it on by signing, *"want computer."*

Manual signing used to be the most commonly used system of communication for people with autism who do not use speech. One reason is that manual signs are totally "portable" and require no external devices to use. However, many people with autism seem to find it easier to use AAC systems that use symbols that are more concrete and permanent than manual signs. For instance, visual-spatial communication symbols such as pictures or line drawings work better for many children with autism. Furthermore, most parents, teachers, and classmates do not understand manual signs, and some children with autism do not have the manual skills (whether fine motor or finger dexterity) that are needed to produce them.

Decisions about whether or not to teach children to use manual signs for output are complicated and should be made by the team of people providing educational supports to your child. Factors to be considered include:

- whether your child can learn signs via imitation or physical prompting,
- your child's degree of motor skill,
- how rapidly he can acquire vocabulary in sign language vs. in other modalities,

- the portability of the system (you can take your hands with you everywhere!) compared to other systems being considered, and
- the likelihood that the signs will be understood by significant others (at school, home, and in the community).

Aided Symbols

Real Objects

The easiest type of aided symbol for most people to learn is a *real object symbol*, a three-dimensional object (or partial object) that stands for an activity, place, or thing. For example, Marcia uses real object symbols to ask for what she wants and to share information with others. If she's thirsty, she brings her teacher a cup to ask for something to drink. If she wants to go out in the car, she brings her mom the car keys. After she goes to the park, she can tell her sister what she did by showing her the Frisbee that she enjoys using there.

For Marcia, the cup, keys, and Frisbee are symbols representing "I'm thirsty," " I want to go out in the car," and "I went to the park." These specific symbols were selected for Marcia because she always drinks from a cup, sees her mom use those keys, and carries the Frisbee to the park. She has learned from experience to associate the symbols with the activities they represent. Limitations of using such objects include their limited portability (which may be improved by use of miniatures) and the risk that they will be unavailable when needed.

Photographs

Photographs are more difficult to learn to use than real object symbols because of their greater symbolic relation to those objects, but can still be very useful. As part of an AAC system, photos may be used to represent specific people, places, activities, or items. For example, Hoa uses photos of food items to ask for her lunch in the high school cafeteria. She can talk to her classmates about her family by using photos of them, and can tell her teachers that she went to San Diego for her holiday by showing postcards and photos of the places she visited.

The advantage of photographs is that they are easier to carry around than are real object symbols. The disadvantage is that they have to be taken with a camera, bought, or cut out of magazines or other media, so they can be time-consuming to produce. Fortunately, recent technological advances have made digital cameras available to most of us (although they remain relatively expensive). These cameras permit computer files of pictures to be stored and modified, using various software programs. Useful photographs can then be readily copied and shared, while those that are not used frequently can simply be deleted. The cost of color printing is now fairly reasonable and may permit colored symbols (both photographic and drawings). However, while color may enhance some children's ability to use a symbol, this is not the case for all children. That is, some children may respond very well to black-and-white photographs (or drawings) early in training.

Line Drawing Symbols

Line drawings may be black-and-white or color illustrations of objects meant to represent people, places, activities, and items, as well as actions (eat, sit, sleep, etc.), feelings (happy, angry, bored, etc.), descriptors (hot, little, up/down, etc.), and social etiquette messages (please, thank you, etc.). Many types of line drawing symbol sets are commercially available in a variety of sizes and forms (including some that permit a printed word on the card) from different companies. The most commonly used line drawing symbols are called Picture Communication Symbols© (PCS), and are available from the Mayer-Johnson Company. They come in a binder with 3,000 symbols that can be photocopied and then glued to a page. A software program called Boardmaker™ can also be used to produce communication displays of PCS symbols.

Alphabet Symbols

The last types of symbols we'll talk about here are alphabet symbols— A, B, C, D, and so forth. We use letters combined into printed words to represent many ideas and things every day— you're using these symbols right now in order to read this book! People with autism who know how to read can also use words and letters to communicate.

Even if a child doesn't know how to read *everything* he needs to communicate, words might be useful to communicate *some* things. For example, Jordan can recognize words for many foods he eats regularly, such as "Kellogg's Rice Krispies" and "peanut butter." He has several pages of these food words in a communication book that he carries around with him. When he wants to ask for something he likes to eat, he simply points to the word in his book.

The advantages of words are that many of them can be placed on a single page, and they are easily understood by people who can read. The disadvantage is that people with autism who cannot read will not be able to use them effectively. It is important to be able to distinguish between *word-calling*—when a child can name a written word—and *comprehension*—when a child can appropriately use a word or act on the word as equivalent to what it represents.

AAC Techniques

Now that you know about unaided and aided symbols, we can talk about what to *do* with those symbols and how they can be used to help a child communicate. Basically, two types of AAC techniques are available: non-electronic or "low tech" and electronic or "high tech."

Non-electronic ("Low Tech") Techniques

Non-electronic or "low tech" techniques include:
- Communication books (for example, these may have cardboard or vinyl covers that permit some pictures

to be shown on the cover while other pictures are stored within the book). Such books may contain symbols to point to or symbols that are attached (e.g., with Velcro™) and can be readily removed, as when using the PECS method described in Chapter 6.

- Communication boards on which pictures are either printed or affixed, and then covered with a clear laminate to protect the pictures from wear.
- Communication wallets (these may contain photographs or other symbols in clear plastic credit card holders).
- Fanny packs (for example, small pouches that can be strapped around the waist and that contain object symbols or other important items).
- Other devices that are neither battery-operated nor computer-based (such as date-books, notepads, Post-it notes, etc.).

Most of us use non-electronic AAC techniques regularly, although we probably don't recognize it! Do you carry a "Daily Planner" to keep track of your appointments? Do you use a grocery list when you shop? Have you ever shared family photographs in your wallet with co-workers or neighbors, or pointed to a picture or foreign word in a menu to order your food in a restaurant? All of these are examples of non-electronic techniques for communication!

Like all AAC techniques, there are both advantages and disadvantages to using "low tech" techniques for communication. The advantages are that they are relatively inexpensive; can be designed so they are easy to transport or carry around; and can be used in flexible, individualized ways. For example, one youngster had a few symbols of outside play equipment attached to a loop that hung on his belt so that he could use his hands freely on the equipment but also choose where he wanted to play next (e.g., on the swings, slide, etc.). The disadvantage is that someone must take responsibility for keeping these AAC systems updated with messages (symbols) that the child needs to communicate. Of course, this is also the case with electronic techniques.

Electronic ("High Tech") Techniques

Numerous *electronic or "high tech"* communication techniques that require some type of external power source (e.g., batteries or electricity) are also available. The primary advantage of electronic communication devices is that they produce output that can be readily understood by almost anyone your child might want to communicate with. Words might be displayed on a screen or printed out on paper, or the device might use voice output. For example, when a child touches a symbol on a voice output device, it "speaks" the message that has been programmed for the symbol.

Some "high tech" devices are quite complex and expensive, while others are relatively simple to program and operate. For example, the BIGmack (AbleNet, Inc.) is a small device with a built-in microswitch, which, when activated, plays a single recorded message up to twenty seconds long. Recording a message into the BIGmack takes only seconds, using the voice of whoever sets up the device. New messages can be recorded over old ones throughout the day. So, for example, with the assistance of an aide who is responsible for recording the messages, a kindergarten-aged student could use a BIGmack to

1. greet his teacher and classmates on arrival at school ("Hi, how are you today?"), then to
2. recite the "Pledge of Allegiance" with his classmates, then to
3. participate in a language arts lesson by "reciting" the repeating line of a story the teacher is reading, and then to
4. call out "Duck, duck, duck, duck, goose!" while a classmate touches each child's head in the circle.

As you can see, the BIGmack might not do very much, but with some creativity and planning, it can be a very useful tool for classroom participation! Additional examples of basic electronic devices include the MessageMate (Words+, Inc.) and Parrot (Zygo Industries, Inc.).

Other devices are capable of delivering more than twenty messages (in some cases, thousands!) and are more difficult both to program and use because they are more complex. Of course, the advantage of such devices is that they can contain a greater number of pre-programmed messages (e.g., "hello," "I need help," "I need a break," "I want to go to the bathroom," etc.). In addition, many of these devices have other features as well, including printers, calculators, large memory capacities for storing lengthy text and speeches, and the ability to interface with standard computers. Some examples include the AlphaTalker and Walker Talker (Prentke Romich Co.); Macaw (Zygo Industries, Inc.); Digivox (Dynavox Systems, Inc.) and Speaking Dynamically (Mayer-Johnson Company). The vast majority of devices today use either digitized human speech or very high quality synthetic speech. The size of the buttons used to activate messages is not an issue since virtually all modern high tech devices allow you to customize them to match the user's motor skills.

Aside from the cost (which can range from less than $200 to more than $10,000!), one of the major disadvantages of electronic devices is that they are more cumbersome and more vulnerable to simple wear and tear than are non-electronic techniques. They can break down (which may require expert repair specialists); their batteries can run down or fail; the switches used to operate them can fail to function; a change in location can make it impractical to transport them; and they require someone to program messages into them on a regular basis.

In addition, it is important to emphasize that having an electronic device does not make a person a good communicator any more than having a basketball makes someone Michael Jordan! Electronic devices are *tools* for communication, and children with autism need to be taught how to use them in meaningful ways, just as they are taught to use other communication techniques. They should *not* be seen as "quick fix" solutions to the communication difficulties these children experience.

What about Computers?

Standard PC and Macintosh computers are "assistive devices" that can be used for a variety of purposes by children with autism. When they are used for AAC, they are essentially electronic techniques that can be used for communication and other purposes, depending on the software. Some children may use portable, battery-operated computers for communication through special software that allows the computer to "talk." Other children may use computers for writing, as learning tools in the classroom or at home, or for entertainment through computer games.

Many children with autism enjoy and benefit from using computers for the same reasons as most children do: computers often provide interesting visual input and output, are predictable, and (most importantly!) are fun to use. However, it is important to choose software programs that encourage them to interact with others rather than isolate themselves for hours on end. For example, many software programs involve two-child games that require turn taking, joint attention, and cooperation. It is also important that children with autism be exposed to a variety of software programs and discouraged from using the same ones over and over again in ritualistic ways. Teaching a child to take turns or interact with peers while using the computer may help counter a child's tendency to play in isolation with some programs. On the downside, of course, computers can be expensive to buy and maintain and are subject to the same "wear and tear" problems as other electronic devices.

Designing an AAC System

Now that you have a basic understanding of the symbol and technique options that are available, we can consider some of the most important decisions that are needed to design an AAC system. These have to do with the types of symbols to be used and the types of messages that will be available for communication.

Symbol Selection

It's important to think carefully about what types of symbol to use with each child, because the same symbols are not necessarily best for everyone. The most important consideration is that the symbols should be easy for the child to learn how to use for communication. The more you know about a child's interactions with pictures and other symbols, the more likely it is that you will make a successful selection. For example, if your child spends time looking at pictures or photographs in books and magazines, then these types of symbols may be easy for him to use within a communication system. If you lay out a group of symbols varying from color photographs to clip art to black-and-white line drawings and notice that your child primarily looks at and picks up the line drawings, then it may be helpful to start with such symbols.

Ultimately, the answer to the question "which type of symbol is best?" will only be answered by observing how readily your child learns to use symbols within a communication system. For example, in Chapter Six you will be introduced to PECS, a system for teaching communication skills to children with autism. Various types of symbols can be introduced through PECS, to see which one(s) your child learns to use most readily.

Messages

Perhaps the most important decision to be made involves what types of messages the child needs to communicate in various contexts. Communicative messages can be divided into four main categories, according to their functions:

1.   wants and needs;
2.   information sharing;
3.   social closeness; and
4.   social etiquette (Light, 1988).

Wants and needs messages are the easiest to learn how to communicate. Young children first communicate about wants and needs when they learn to say things like: "I want _____;

"Give me _____;" and "I don't want _____." Both non-electronic and electronic communication devices should contain symbols that the child can use to make requests for food, activities, desired items, and people. There should also be symbols that allow the child to say "no," ask for a break, ask for help, and ask to be left alone.

Information sharing messages enable the child to share information with classmates, teachers, family members, and others. For example, most parents ask their children, "What did you do at school today?" when they come home after school. In addition, children often have a need to exchange more complicated information, such as when they want to ask or answer questions in class. Symbols that correspond to the vocabulary of the lesson (e.g., animals when talking about the zoo, symbols related to the holiday of the month, etc.) can help children share information and allow them to participate in these types of interactions.

Often, the purpose of communication is not to get what we want or to share information—it's simply to connect with other people and enjoy each other. Children with autism also need to be able to have such **social closeness** interactions. They need to be able to get the attention of others, interact in positive ways, and use humor to connect to other people. At least some of the symbols in their communication systems should be related to messages for social closeness (e.g., "Let's go play!" "That was great!" "I love you," etc.).

Finally, a fourth purpose of communication has to do with the routines for **social etiquette** that are important in specific cultures. In North America, for example, people are expected to say "please," "thank you," and "excuse me" in certain situations. It's also considered polite to say "hello" or "goodbye" when meeting or leaving someone and to shake someone's hand if it's offered. Students who use communication displays need to be provided with symbols that enable them to interact with others in ways that are culturally acceptable and respectful.

How can you determine exactly which messages from these four categories should be included on a display? Some questions to consider include:

- *Which messages will your child need to communicate on a regular basis (e.g., daily) or frequently (e.g., several times in a day)?* Some examples might include greetings, requests for help, "yes," "no," requests related to basic wants and needs (bathroom, water, food, etc.), and social etiquette messages (e.g., "please," "thank you").

- *Which messages will facilitate participation (e.g., information sharing) in family or school activities?* For example, a second grader might tell his mother what he did at school today by showing her "remnants" of various activities, such as paper scraps from his art project or the flyer he got at the school assembly.

- *Which messages will enable your child to participate in social interactions?* For example, a high school student at a pep rally might need a message in his BigMACK that says "Go, team, go!" Or, children of any age might want to talk about their family; fun events they did in the past; and favorite topics such as basketball stars or cars by using a scrapbook with photographs, cards, magazine pictures, and remnants that represent motivating topics.

You can see from these guidelines that most children will probably need to communicate dozens of messages each day. Initially, it is important to start by teaching the child to use symbols for the most motivating messages. However, it is important not to limit communication only to concrete "wants and needs" messages, such as *eat, drink, toilet, juice, cookie, puzzle,* and so forth. How boring! The communication system must be able to accommodate a sufficiently large number of messages to meet students' social, learning, and other needs as well.

Teaching Your Child to Use His AAC System

The first step in introducing an AAC system is for family members and professionals to meet to discuss your child's current communication, motor, and learning skills and any specific deficits. This information will help in choosing and designing an appropriate AAC system. Each team member will make unique contributions to this decision based on his or her own knowledge of, and interactions with, your child. If your child is in a school-age, preschool, or early intervention program, this team should include the parents, the child, the teacher, the speech-language pathologist, other related service providers, a psychologist and/or learning consultant, and an administrator.

Once your child's needs have been identified, the service agency will work with you, the parents, to identify what the agency will provide in order to meet these needs. The team members develop a plan for acquiring the necessary materials for introducing the communication system and for teaching your child to use it. Together, the team members create annual measurable goals for learning to use the AAC system and develop strategies that will be most effective in realizing those goals. The team also will develop measurable intermediate steps (benchmarks) that will help the team members monitor progress throughout the next six months to a year. All of this information is included in your child's Individualized Education Program (IEP) or Individualized Family Service Plan (IFSP). The following are some examples of annual goals and benchmarks:

> **Annual Goal:** Kim will request desired items from adults and peers.
>
> **Benchmark 1:** Upon seeing a desired item, Kim will approach an adult, activate a single-picture message on her communication device at least twenty times per school day without prompting.
>
> **Benchmark 2:** In a group art activity, Kim will ask a classmate for two items necessary for the project with no prompting during three of three *art activities*.

The IEP and/or IFSP includes a description of who must do what, when, and where. In many cases, the speech-language pathologist will be the professional "in charge" of your child's AAC system. This means that he might be the one who determines which vocabulary to teach your child, and teaches your child how and in what situations to access the vocabulary, etc.

The speech-language pathologist also interacts with all other team members—including family members—to make sure that your child is using his AAC system as effectively as possible in all environments. Just as the "plan" for developing AAC should be created by a team, it should also be implemented by a team. For your child to become a successful communicator, it is imperative that everyone who interacts with his:

- knows how his AAC system works (how he turns on the electronic device and accesses the vocabulary, what his manual signs mean, or what the pictures he uses mean),
- expects him to communicate with them by creating situations in which communication will be necessary,
- makes recommendations to the person "in charge" as to what additional steps must be taken to maximize the effectiveness of the AAC system. This includes ensuring that your child has the opportunity to interact with peers during a variety of activities, and that there is not just one "interpreter" in the classroom who understands what your child is communicating.

Finally...

As you can see, there are many issues to consider when designing a communication system for a child with autism. You need to think about the types of symbols you will use, the messages that need to be conveyed, and many other factors. It can be overwhelming if you think that you have to "get it just right" from the very beginning. The truth is that even the most experienced communication system designers often need to experiment with various options before they find the best solution for a particular child. So, don't be discouraged, and remember—helping a child who cannot speak to communicate is probably THE most valuable gift you can offer!

References & Resources

(Note: All of these publications, except for those by Bloomberg & Johnson and Weiss & Harris, were written for a professional audience.)

Augmentative and Alternative Communication. Quarterly professional journal. Decker Publishing, Inc., One James St. South, P. O. Box 620, L. C. D. 1, Hamilton, Ontario L8N 3K7 CANADA.

Beukelman, D. & Mirenda, P. (1998). *Augmentative and alternative communication: Management of severe communication disorders in children and adults (2nd ed).* Baltimore: Paul H. Brookes.

Bloomberg, K. & Johnson, H. (1991). *Communication without speech.* Victoria, Australia: ACER.

Calculator, S. & Jorgensen, C. (1994). *Including students with severe disabilities in schools: Fostering communication, interaction, and participation.* San Diego: Singular Publishing.

Glennen, S.L. & DeCoste, D. (1997). *The handbook of augmentative and alternative communication.* San Diego: Singular Publishing Group.

Heckaman, K.A., Alber, S., Hooper, S., & Heward, W. (1998). A comparison of least-to-most prompts and progressive time delay on the disruptive behavior of students with autism. *Journal of Behavioral Education, 8,* 171-201.

Johnson, J., Baumgart, D., Helmstetter, E., & Curry, C. (1996). *Augmenting basic communication in natural contexts.* Baltimore: Paul H. Brookes.

Layton, T. & Watson, L. (1995). Enhancing communication in nonverbal children with autism. In K.A. Quill (Ed.), *Teaching children with autism: Strategies to enhance communication and socialization* (pp. 73-1010). New York: Delmar Publication.

Light, J. & Binger, C. (1998). *Building communicative competence with individuals who use augmentative and alternative communication.* Baltimore: Paul H. Brookes.

Lloyd, L.L., Fuller, D., & Arvidson, H. (Eds.), *Augmentative and alternative communication: Principles and practice.* Needham Heights, MA: Allyn & Bacon.

Romski, M.A. & Sevcik, R.A. (1996). *Breaking the speech barrier: Language development through augmented means.* Baltimore: Paul H. Brookes.

Siegel-Causey, E. & Guess, D. (1989). *Enhancing nonsymbolic communication interactions among learners with severe disabilities.* Baltimore: Paul H. Brookes.

Stone, W.L., Ousley, O.Y., & Littleford, C.D. (1997). Motor imitation in young children with autism: What's the object? *Journal of Abnormal Child Psychology, 25,* 475-485.

Stone, W.L., Ousley, O.Y., Yoder, P.J., Hogan, K.L. & Hepburn, S.L. (1997). Nonverbal communication in 2- and 3-year old children with autism. *Journal of Autism and Developmental Disorders, 27,* 677-696.

Weiss, M.J. & Harris, S.L. (2001). *Reaching out, joining in: Teaching social skills to young children with autism.* Bethesda, MD: Woodbine House.

6 | The Picture Exchange Communication System (PECS): Initial Training

When I first met Anne, she was three years old and had just been diagnosed with autism. She had no speech or formal communication skills. She clearly liked snacks and juice as evidenced by her taking chips and sips of orange juice when these were left on a table. If I held a chip in my hand, she looked at the chip and reached for it. If I gently closed my fingers around the chip, she would pry my fingers open to get to the chip. Whenever she took things that I held she looked at the item and never at my eyes. If I held the chip tightly, she began to cry. If she saw a chip or a cup on a bookshelf too high for her to reach she cried and fell to the floor. She also liked to watch a particular cartoon videotape. If the tape were turned off, she did not turn to her parents or other adults but walked to the TV and began to cry and slap her head.

Everyone was concerned that Anne's tantrums were increasing in number and in severity. We assessed that she did not imitate simple actions or repeat simple sounds or words. We taught her to use PECS whenever we noticed there was something that she wanted. Within two days, she could pick up a picture, reach across a tabletop, and put it in the open hand of the person who held the item she wanted. Within a week, if the TV were turned off, she picked up a picture of her favorite videotape and gave it to her mother sitting next to her. Everyone noticed how much calmer she now appeared and how much more time she now spent going to her parents. At this point, she still was not a good imitator nor had she used any spoken words, but she clearly had mastered the first step in functional communication—she had found her audience!

Many young children with autism (i.e., those under five years of age) do not use speech or other forms of formal communication when they enter educational or treatment programs. When a child does not speak, of course our hope is for that child to learn to speak as quickly as possible. However, as we discussed in our earlier chapter on communication, a critical problem for such children is their lack of communication skills in any modality. Furthermore, we also know that young children with autism often are very poor imitators of actions and speech when they are first diagnosed. An important question is: Are there ways to rapidly help a child learn to communicate that do not require speech or imitation? Fortunately, the answer is yes.

One method is to use the Picture Exchange Communication System (PECS), which we describe in this chapter in some detail. We developed this system (Bondy & Frost, 1994; Frost & Bondy, 1994; Frost & Bondy, 2001) over a period of time and primarily with young children with autism. We provide details on how to begin the system and how best to develop more complex communication skills. Many of the training strategies described can and should be incorporated into teaching the use of any AAC system.

The Development of PECS

Over a dozen years ago, we were working on communication skills with a young boy with autism who was not successful at vocal imitation or pointing to pictures. We had tried teaching him to point to a picture among an array of pictures that corresponded to things he liked. However, we encountered a number of problems with this approach. First, in part due to his young age, he had difficulty reliably using just one finger to touch one picture. In addition, at times he would touch a picture when his eyes were focused on something happening outside. We weren't sure if he really wanted what he was pointing to, if he wanted what he was looking at outside the window, or if he simply liked the sound of his finger tapping on the picture board.

We were also concerned about our observation that some children with autism had been taught to point to pictures when they wanted something but had not been taught to approach someone. That is, they could be sitting in the back of the room pointing to a picture on their communication board, but unless someone happened to be looking at them, their pointing would be ineffective. They had learned to point to pictures, not to communicate with people.

Finally, we were concerned about the strategy traditionally used to teach children to point to pictures. Like others in the field, we had tried to teach children to match a picture with an object that we displayed. We would hold up an item, such as a ball, issue a simple instruction (i.e., "match" or "find the same"), and teach the child to point to the corresponding picture. Many professionals advised that prior to teaching matching pictures to objects, we had to be sure that the child could match objects to objects. In each of these types of matching lessons, it was the teacher who started the interaction, not the child. Some children would only point to a picture when we began the sequence by holding up an item or using a spoken instruction. Therefore, these children were dependent upon various prompts from adults to communicate and could not initiate an interaction.

Since the boy we were working with could not reliably imitate our actions, we had to devise a method to teach him to functionally communicate without imitating us. We thought this might be possible based on our knowledge that very young children typically learn to communicate independent of imitating others. That is, they learn to approach adults and engage in actions that are communicative, but are not refined or formalized messages. (For example, an eighteen-month-old girl might look at her mother and simultaneously reach toward her ball that fell onto the floor.)

Given these concerns, we decided to teach this child to give us a single picture that corresponded to the item she currently desired.

As with typical communication, she would need to approach us to give us her picture (message). We started by making a line drawing of a pretzel, which was something we knew she enjoyed eating. With one of us enticing her with pretzels and the other one helping her with hand-over-hand guidance, we gradually taught her to give this picture in exchange for the pretzel. Over time, we reduced the physical prompting and added pictures of other items and activities she desired to his "vocabulary." Eventually we taught her to place several pictures in a row to construct a sentence.

We started using this same method to teach other young children with autism to communicate, and, in time, named our method the Picture Exchange Communication System (PECS). Our hope was that this method would accomplish several things:

1. The child would initiate the communication (rather than depend on a cue from the adult).
2. The child would find a communicative partner and approach that partner.
3. The child would use a single picture and avoid confusion about the intent of the message.

We also hoped that this method of communication would avoid certain potential problems:

1. The child would not have to depend on prompts from the adult.
2. The child would not need to have learned to imitate actions or words prior to starting this lesson.
3. The child would not have to learn to make eye contact on demand prior to starting this lesson.
4. The child did not have to learn to sit quietly in a chair prior to starting this lesson.
5. The child would quickly learn to communicate rather than initially learning to match pictures to objects.

Of course, ultimately it is important for children to learn to imitate actions, sounds, and words, to sit attentively in a chair, and to look at someone on request. However, these are not prerequisites for a child to learn to functionally communicate her wants and desires. To functionally communicate, it is necessary for a child to approach someone and then deliver a message. And this is something that PECS most definitely enables many children (and adults) with autism to do.

In this chapter, we will describe the basic sequence of training in the initial steps of the Picture Exchange Communication System (PECS) in some detail. Many of these teaching strategies are very effective in teaching children with autism other AAC techniques or speech. The next chapter will cover more advanced and complex lessons.

What Are the Prerequisites for Starting PECS?

The primary factor to consider before beginning PECS is what your child does (e.g., reaches for, moves toward something) to indicate what is reinforcing to her. If a child reaches for snacks, toys, trinkets, or other small items, then we are confident that we can teach her to reach for a picture instead of reaching for the item.

Your child does *not* need to have wonderful fine motor skills. If she has trouble picking up small items, the picture can be modified so that it is easier to manipulate. For example, the picture can be glued to a wooden or foam block or a dowel, to aid in picking it up. The size of the picture can be modified as well to help in manipulation.

Neither does your child have to know the meaning of the picture before starting PECS. Our aim in the first part of PECS is to teach the child to initiate an interaction with another person, so there is no reason to precede teaching the exchange by trying to teach the meaning of the picture. Not until the third phase of PECS training (covered later in this chapter) do we focus on assuring that users are able to select distinct messages.

We are not aware of any cognitive prerequisites indicated by scores on a standardized developmental test. That is, children do not have to reach a minimum developmental age before they can successfully learn PECS. Instead, it is critical to observe that the child can clearly indicate (such as by reaching for a toy) what is reinforcing to her in a form that can ultimately be modified to manipulating a physical symbol, such as a picture.

Skills such as eye-to-eye contact, sitting quietly in a chair, responding to a series of simple instructions, or being able to match pictures to objects or other pictures are *not* prerequisites for PECS.

Finally, a child does not have to be nonverbal to benefit from PECS. The primary focus during the first phase of PECS is on teaching communicative initiation. Therefore, while PECS is frequently used with children who have no spoken words, it has also been used effectively with children who say some words but do not initiate with those words.

What Are the Phases of Teaching PECS?

We've broken the sequence of steps to learn in PECS into six phases. In the first phase, children are taught to initiate communication. The second phase expands the use of pictures to other people, places, and rewards. In the third phase, making specific choices between pictures is addressed. The fourth phase teaches the child to construct simple sentences. At this point, we also begin to teach children to be more specific about what they want by teaching them how to use attributes to qualify their requests. The fifth phase assures that children can respond to the direct question, "What do you want?" while the sixth phase teaches children to comment about various items and activities. This chapter covers Phases One through Four, and Chapter 7 continues with Phases Five and Six.

How to Begin Teaching PECS

Before we can begin to teach a child to communicate, there must be a reason for that child to communicate. In Chapter One, we noted two broad reasons to communicate: 1) to receive concrete objects, events, or actions; and 2) to receive social rewards, such as attention or praise. For very young children with autism, we have found that social rewards are not very effective motivators. Therefore, it will be more effective to teach communication about things you know your child likes.

Determining What Is Rewarding to Your Child

Before you can formally begin teaching PECS to your child, you need to determine what she likes—that is, to list a number of potentially reinforcing items or rewards.

To do this type of reinforcer assessment, we first systematically observe what a child does. We do not need to be able to formally communicate with the child. While it would certainly be helpful to simply ask the child, "What do you like?" we can learn the answer by several other methods. First, we could ask the child's parents and other caregivers about the child's preferences. We also could carefully set up various situations and watch the child's actions. For example, we could simply hold a piece of candy in our open hand (or place it on a table) and observe whether or not the child takes the candy. We could also place several toys on a tabletop and observe which ones the child plays with (whether appropriately or in some unique fashion). We also can observe what the child tends to spend a lot of time doing—we assume, for instance, that a child who stacks blocks over and over likes blocks.

Ideally, we will find a set of items that the child likes. We will also try to assure that not all items are types of food or drink. If all of her experiences involving PECS (or any other communication system) are linked only to snacks, then she will limit her use of communication skills to times when these snacks are available but not in other situations. In order for her to learn to use her new skill in a variety of settings, we must carefully plan to quickly introduce an array of opportunities to communicate.

Next, it is helpful to prioritize those items in a hierarchy. We now present the child with a choice between a pair of items. For example, we could place a candy in one hand and a simple toy in our other hand, and observe which one the child reliably takes over a series of presentations. By pairing the candy with various items, we might determine that the child always selects candy as compared with other items. We would next try this same type of comparison to determine the priority of other items offered to the child. We suggest continuing this prioritizing until you find items that your child clearly does not like—those she pushes away. Such items will be important when you want to teach your child to calmly reject some items or when you want to be certain of her choice between two items (e.g., "She likes candy but she hates pickles!").

During this preference assessment period, it is important to also assess how much effort your child is willing to put into obtaining whatever it is you are offering. If your child puts out little effort to obtain reinforcing items directly, she is not likely to put in more effort to obtain pictures corresponding to those items. Therefore, if your child seems very passive or puts little energy into obtaining items, then we suggest first working on helping her show more definitely what she wants before you teach her to use PECS. Such effort could involve walking several feet to obtain something in view, prying open someone's fingers holding an item, or pushing aside a covering that is partially hiding a desired item.

When trying to figure out what is reinforcing for some children it will be helpful to look at when they protest. For example, your child may not actively approach the TV, but may watch it if a cartoon-video is playing. Even more importantly, if you turn the TV off, she may begin to whine and look around as if searching for what went wrong. Now is the time to begin a lesson because now she is most motivated to watch TV.

Phase One: Initiating Communication

The first step in PECS is to teach your child to initiate a request. Teaching strategies that require imitation or matching-to-sample as prerequisite skills often address spontaneous communication after children can imitate or respond to direct questions such as, "What do you want?" or "What is this?" We believe it is very important to teach children to be spontaneous communicators as quickly as possible, so initiation is the first goal of PECS.

Once you have found a powerful incentive as described above, you can introduce your child to PECS by teaching her to pick up and exchange a picture that corresponds to the item she wants. (See the sidebar on page 79 for information on making the picture.) First, you must ensure that your child will want the item when you are ready to begin teaching PECS. To increase the likelihood that she will, withhold the item from her for a period of time so that she comes to "miss" it. Then when you show her the item, she will be motivated to obtain it. Other strategies for enhancing your child's desire to gain access to an item are described in Table 6-1.

When the first PECS lesson is started, your child's focus will be on the enticing item. How do we teach her to pick up the *picture* of the item? When we first tried this lesson, we tried the natural approach—the person who was holding the enticing item also physically assisted the child in picking up the picture and giving it to the person holding the item. We noticed several problems with this approach. One, if I held an item up to the child and I used my other hand to help guide the child to pick up the picture, I was out of hands to receive the picture from the child! But more importantly, we found that if the person enticing was also the one helping, then the child tended to simply wait for the help. The solution that we use involves having two people helping at this point in training.

One person is directly in front of the child and entices her with something desirable, as described in Table 6-1 on the next two pages. This person (whom we call the "communicative partner") uses no verbal prompts, thus avoiding simple questions or cues such as, "What do you want?" or "Give me the picture." These prompts would tend to teach the child to wait for the question to be asked before responding. Furthermore, there is no reason to ask the question because we can interpret the child's reach as

Table 6-1 | Communication Enhancement Strategies

1. Make favorite items inaccessible.	Place your child's favorite items out of reach but within view. Put the items on a high shelf, on a counter top, in clear containers with tight lids, etc. Don't automatically offer items.
2. Give small portions.	At meals or at snack time, offer bite-sized or small portions. Cut up a sandwich and give only part of it at a time. Put one or two swallows of a drink in a cup at a time. Help your child to understand that more is available by giving subtle cues such as saying "We have more juice," or by showing the food/drink item.
3. Consume a portion of a favorite food/drink in front of your child.	In view of your child, eat or drink a portion of the item of yours she really wants. Show your extreme pleasure at being able to consume the item ("Boy, is this JUICE good!!!")
4. Create the need for assistance.	Give your child access to a favorite item that he/she needs your assistance to enjoy. Encourage your child to seek assistance from you to wind the toy; turn on the TV, radio, tape recorder, or something; open a container, etc.
5. Interrupt a favorite cooperative activity.	Begin a favorite activity that you and your child both participate in. Once you are both enjoying yourselves, stop the activity and encourage your child to signal to you that he/she wants to continue. For example, while pushing your child on the swing, stop her/him in mid-air.
6. Offer your child something that he/she does not like.	Offer your child a non-preferred item/activity and encourage him/her to tell you "no" in an appropriate way.

7. Offer a choice.	Hold out two favorite items and say nothing. Expect your child to let you know which one he/she wants.
8. Violate your child's expectations.	Start putting together a puzzle with your child. After she has put in three or four pieces, give her a piece that obviously does not fit.
9. Surprise your child.	"Accidentally" spill, drop, or break something. Gasp and look at the "mess" and then at your child. Wait for a reaction.

*For a complete list of "Communicative Temptations," see:
Wetherby, A.M. & Prizant, B.M. (1989).The expression of communicative intent: Assessment guidelines. *Seminars in Speech and Language,* 10, 77-91.

When using any of these strategies, once your child has initiated an interest in the item (looking at it, moving toward it, reaching for it, taking you to it), PAUSE and WAIT. DO NOT immediately prompt a response from your child (Do not ask "What do you want?" or say "Say, _____."), as this will likely result in imitation, direction following, or question responding. Waiting will enhance the likelihood that your child will spontaneously communicate with you!! Wait at least five seconds with an expectant look, raised shoulders, raised eyebrows, and then if your child has not responded, provide subtle prompts. These could include gesturing to his/her communication book, saying the initial sound of the word, or having a second person MODEL the response. Another technique is to say a "carrier phrase." For example, slowly say to your child "I want" and then pause expectantly after saying "want" and wait for your child to "fill in the blank."

indicating what the child wants. When the child reaches for the enticing item, the second person, sitting or standing behind the child, guides the child to:

1. pick up the picture (with whatever physical assistance is necessary),
2. reach toward the first person, and
3. place the picture in the open hand of the first person. The communicative partner immediately gives the child the item while saying the name of the item (see photo below).

(For more detailed instructions about completing these steps, see "Designing Effective Phase 1 and Phase 2 Lessons" at the end of this chapter.)

The role of the second person, the physical prompter, is (in this lesson) to reduce the physical assistance as quickly as possible. This reduction in help is best accomplished by using a strategy that at first glance seems backwards! That is, the physical prompter provides physical help for picking up and reaching while eliminating assistance for letting go of the picture. Then, help is

What Symbols Can Be Used with PECS?

As noted in the previous chapter, there are many symbols that can be incorporated into an alternative or augmentative communication system. We may use photographs, line drawings, product logos, or three-dimensional or miniaturized representations (such as kitchen-magnets or actual items covered with resin). These symbols may be in black and white or color. Any of these types of symbols may be used in PECS as long as the child can easily manipulate them.

For some children, covering the picture with a laminate or contact paper will sufficiently protect the picture for repeated use and permit placement of material (such as Velcro™) to assist in attaching the symbol to a communication book. The backing of the symbol may need to be bolstered for some children. This support can be provided by thicker paper or cardboard, thin wood, plastic, or even metal (as from the lid of a frozen juice container). When a child has physical difficulty in picking up or holding a picture, modifications of the symbol can be made via extensions (e.g., a wooden dowel attached to the symbol) or by placing the symbol on a vertical vs. slanted board, providing a better angle for the child to grasp the symbol.

given for picking up the picture but eliminated (often in small increments over several opportunities) for reaching across to the open hand. This reduction in physical assistance can include changing the point of contact from the child's hand, to wrist, to elbow, etc. Finally, help is eliminated for picking up the picture.

How quickly this help can be eliminated depends on a number of factors, including how motivated the child is to obtain the item and how skilled the physical prompter is at providing and reducing assistance. The physical prompter can be a professional, a relative, or even another child as long as he or she has demonstrated effective use of this teaching strategy.

Some children with autism have learned this first phase of PECS within a few minutes, while other children have taken several days. You should gear the length of your teaching sessions to your child's degree of motivation. We certainly do not want the lesson to run until she no longer wants the item we are using to entice her—otherwise, we would be trying to make a child ask for something she doesn't want! Therefore, it is difficult to predetermine exactly how many opportunities to insist on. We try to end the session while the child is being successful and still wants the item we are using, knowing we will set up other opportunities across the day.

A time will come when you do not want to give your child everything she asks for every time she asks! Maybe you have run out of the requested item, or it is not yet time for the requested activity. In any event, you will need to say "no" to your child sometimes. We will describe several different ways to handle this situation in Chapter 7.

Keeping the Rewards Rewarding

As mentioned above, your teaching will become ineffective if your child is no longer interested in the reward you are using to entice communication. It is therefore important to carefully choose rewards, as well as to make sure they remain rewarding for your child.

Some potential rewards are quickly consumed. For example, snack items and beverages disappear once the child eats or drinks. In similar fashion, bubbles, stickers, wind-up toys, electronic devices (especially if you control the remote!), or tops also tend to disappear or stop working on their own. When a child has requested and consumed these kinds of items, she will most likely want another similar item. In general, it is helpful to start with such consumable items, as long as they are not all foods or drinks.

On the other hand, there are some rewards that a child may keep. Such items could include a favorite toy, doll, book, or similar material item. In this case, once the child has been given the item requested, how do we entice the child to make another request?

There are two strategies that can help. For some children, collecting more of their favorite item is still enticing. For example, a child who likes marbles may well be motivated to request other marbles after she has been given one following her request. This way, she can accumulate many marbles. The second strategy involves recovering the item by simply taking it from the child. In this case, we do not ask for the item, as that could involve a new lesson. Rather, we may say, "My turn" (merely to be polite) as we take the item back. If the child appears somewhat upset, another request is likely to follow as long as the physical prompter is ready to assist. Of course, if the child becomes so upset that she begins to severely tantrum, hurting herself or others, the lesson should stop. For this child, we would advise using a more "consumable" item for this part of the training until she has learned to reliably exchange a picture for a desired item.

Phase Two: Expanding the Use of Pictures

The next step in PECS training involves introducing more realistic aspects of communication. For example, during the initial session, we are positioned immediately in front of the child and all she has to do is extend her arm to reach her communicative partner with the picture. Obviously, this arrangement is not typical of the real world. Therefore, the communicative partner must begin to gradually move away from the child in order to foster greater persistence on her part. In a similar vein, the initial lesson begins with the picture immediately in front of the child. This, too, is not typical of the real world. In this case, we must begin to move the picture further from the child but still in plain sight so that she will expend more effort to obtain the picture to bring to the teacher.

At this point in teaching, we introduce a communication binder for the child. This may be a three-ring binder that has a square of Velcro affixed to the middle of the front cover. A single picture used to communicate is displayed on the outside of this binder (placed there by the teacher), while other pictures can be stored within (see photo on next page). The child's family or teacher makes sure that the appropriate picture is on the front of the book depending on the current activity or interests of the child. This binder will help the child identify her own set of pictures, as well as provide a location to place all the pictures she eventually may use.

During this second phase of PECS instruction, we expand the number of motivational items. For example, if we used candy as the first reward in the PECS lesson, then we must introduce other items. In this case, it will be important to add items that are not similar to the first item—that is, something other than food. We may use a favorite toy or access to music or the TV. We must keep in mind that our goal is to teach the child how to initiate functional communication in all situations in which she desires something, rather than as the system used only during snack- or mealtime.

In summary, the goal of this second part of teaching PECS is to increase:

1. the distance from the child to the communicative partner,
2. the distance from the child to the pictures, and
3. the number of items that the child can request.

These goals are accomplished while assuring that only one picture is placed on the front of the communication binder at a time.

Why are there no choices of pictures at this point in training? The key to the first part in PECS training is to teach the child to approach an adult in a situation in which there is something the child wants or needs. Recall that in typical language development, children learn to approach adults to communicate even before they have any formal message (i.e., words) to use. The goal in PECS is to achieve the same spontaneous approach even if the child has yet to learn to be selective about messages. Just as children with no speech delays do, children learning PECS will learn to clarify their message after they have learned to communicatively approach someone.

Phase Three: Choosing the Message within PECS

Once children have learned the essence of communication— finding someone to communicate with— they then are ready to learn how to select specific messages. This involves learning to discriminate between pictures.

In teaching a child to discriminate between pictures, we need to individualize the teaching strategies as well as the type of symbols (i.e., photographs, line drawings, etc.) used. Although these issues are often entwined pragmatically, we will discuss teaching strategies before we describe message selection issues. Throughout the description of these teaching strategies, we will refer to the symbols as "pictures."

Teaching Strategies for Message Selection

Life would be considerably simpler if there were one perfect teaching strategy to help children select from a choice of messages. In our experience, we have found instead that there are a number of helpful techniques to help children learn to discriminate between symbols. We will discuss some of the primary options, but strongly suggest readers look at the references provided at the end of the chapter for a more complete description of discrimination techniques.

During the first two phases of PECS training, children are presented with only one picture at a time. With only one picture to choose from, there is no way of knowing whether the child is connecting the symbol depicted with the item she is requesting. When we begin discrimination training, we place a second picture on the communication book in order to make sure the child understands how the pictures are related to specific items. To begin with, one picture will be associated with something that the child greatly prefers. There are several options for selecting the second picture (the distracter picture). The distracter picture can be either 1) a picture of something neutral or of something the child dislikes, or 2) a picture that looks distinctly different from the picture of the preferred item.

Using Pictures of Neutral or Disliked Items as Distractors. Using this option, you choose a distractor picture that is associated with something that is either neutral (something boring such as a tissue, a piece of paper, etc.) or something that your child clearly doesn't like (pickles, lemons, etc.). You must determine which items are non-preferred or disliked for your child. Children's dislikes are as unique and individual as are their preferences. This strategy focuses on maximizing the difference in the value of each item for your child.

If we use this picture arrangement (one picture of something preferred and the other picture of something non-preferred or disliked), we give the child the corresponding item when she gives us a picture. For example, if the choice is between candy and a wooden spoon, if the child gives the candy picture, we provide candy; if the child gives the spoon picture, we give her the spoon. This strategy generally is successful if the child appears to be somewhat upset if handed the spoon. That is, if the child gave us the spoon picture and then pushed away the of-fered spoon, she is more likely to pay attention to the pictures the next time to assure getting candy rather than the spoon. How-ever, if the child calmly accepts the spoon and even begins to play with it, this strategy will not help her be more careful in selecting pictures. In this case, choose another second item—something that the child is more likely to object to receiving!

Using Distinctly Different Pictures as Distractors. You can also choose a distractor picture that looks very different than the first picture. For example, the second picture can be com-pletely blank. Thus, the choice is between a picture of the item the child likes and a second picture that is simply white. This strategy maximizes the visual differences between the two pic-tures. There are several other ways to emphasize the visual dif-ferences between two pictures, including:

1. color of the item (e.g., one picture is black and white and the other is in color),
2. color of background (e.g., the background of one picture is white and the background of the other picture is yellow),
3. size (e.g., one picture is very large and the other is very small).

In each case, the distractor picture should be of an item your child does not prefer.

If you use this type of strategy, then you must quickly but gradually eliminate the prompt provided to help your child. For example, if your child can reliably select the regular picture when paired with a blank distracter, then you must make the blank card gradually more similar to other pictures. On the other hand, if you used differing colored backgrounds to help the child make selections, then we must gradually make those backgrounds the same. Whichever prompt you introduce to help your child make correct selections, you must gradually remove so that your child learns to select pictures solely because of the contents of the pic-tures themselves.

Note: At this stage of PECS training, only one trainer will be needed, since your child should be able to initiate communication without physical assistance at this point.

General Issues Associated with Successful Discrimination Training

Whichever discrimination training strategy is used, several broad issues must be systematically addressed:

1. how and when to provide feedback,
2. how to correct errors, and
3. making sure the child can discriminate between two desired items.

Providing Feedback. In the first part of PECS, we wait until the child has given us the picture before we respond by providing whatever the child requested. However, in discrimina-

tion training, we now are focused on teaching the child to *select* the correct picture, since she has previously learned to hand us a single picture. Therefore, we have found that providing some vocal (as in, voicing "Oh!") or visual (as in, showing the desired item) feedback at the point of picture selection can hasten the acquisition of this skill. These cues signal the child that she will soon receive what she's asked for. While we may respond vocally as the child selects a picture, we only provide the item when she puts the picture into our hand.

Responding to Errors. Another general issue is how to react to the errors that children may make at this point in training. How should we respond to the child who rejects being handed the non-preferred item? How should we respond to errors within a lesson? The key is to recognize the difference between fixing the problem (which does not lead to new skills) and arranging to teach the appropriate response. For example, if we point to the right picture after the child has made an error, she is likely to pick up and give us that picture, thus appearing to fix the problem. However, in this lesson, she is supposed to be learning to select a picture from a pair of pictures, not take a picture pointed to by the teacher. It is important to respond to errors using a consistent strategy rather than simply repeat the sequence and risking repeating the errors. Remember, there is no one perfect way to teach discrimination, so you must be ready to systematically evaluate alternative strategies. For more information about error correction strategies see Bondy and Sulzer-Azaroff (2001) or Lovaas (1981).

Discriminating Between Pictures of Two Desired Items. Once a child has learned to successfully select from an array of two pictures, we gradually add more pictures. As more pictures are included, we begin to offer the child a choice between items that are more and more similar in preference. In time, the choice may be between two types of cookies or two types of chips. In such cases, how do we know what the child truly desires?

When we offer two equally preferred items, we seek to determine whether there is correspondence between what the child requests and what item the child wants. Therefore, in situations where both (or many) items are enjoyed, when the child gives us a picture, we say, "OK, take it!" Then we watch the child to be certain that she takes the item that was requested. If she reaches for the chocolate cookie after giving us the vanilla cookie picture, then we assume an error was made. We also assume the child really wants the chocolate cookie (since that was the item she reached for), so we teach her to select the chocolate picture in order to take that type of cookie. Here, too, if an error is made, a systematic error correction strategy must be used.

Once a child can discriminate between two pictures, we present her with three, then four, then five pictures representing preferred items. We periodically "check" the child's accuracy by having her "Go get" what she asked for. Eventually, the student learns to discriminate from among all pictures on the cover of and in her communication book.

Progressing to More Symbolic Pictures. Some children need to use three-dimensional or miniaturized representations of items rather than pictures in the beginning of PECS training. As their vocabulary grows, it may be important to try to replace the three-dimensional objects with less bulky two-dimensional symbols. The following example provides clarification on this point as well as suggesting the flexibility we all must provide to some children.

Jeremy was eight years old and had successfully learned the first steps of PECS. However, when his teacher and I began to work on discrimination, we encountered numerous problems. Finally, we found that if we used three-dimensional items covered with an epoxy-resin (from a product called Pour-On™), he gradually became successful at discriminating among sixty symbols. However, his communication book was now very large and bulky, and Jeremy was having difficulty carrying it!

We began to place a small picture of the item on the lower left portion of his resin-encased, three-dimensional symbols. At first, these pictures covered about ten percent of the total surface of the symbol. Even this small change initially resulted in a modest reduction of his discrimination accuracy, but that soon recovered. At that point, we covered a somewhat larger portion of the encased-symbol with a slightly larger picture. Again, even though the change looked minor to us, Jeremy's performance dropped before once more recov-

ering. Over the next few months, we continued to cover his encased-symbols with pictures until, finally, he was able to discriminate all of his symbols using pictures alone. As we added new vocabulary, we generally first had to introduce the symbol with a three-dimensional symbol before gradually replacing it with a picture. (See Frost & Scholefield, 1996, for details.)

Phase Four: Introducing Sentence Structure within PECS

One day, my sixteen-month-old daughter came to me and said, "Doggie!" while pointing to our dog running in the yard. Later that same day, she came over and again said, "Doggie?" but in a manner that led me to believe she was looking for her favorite stuffed animal. Even though she used the same word, she was able to make it clear when she was commenting about something as opposed to when she wanted something. Her tone of voice, including inflection, prosody or rhythm, and other qualities of voice were the cues I used to better understand her message.

When children developing typical language are at a stage when they use only one word at a time, they are still able to alter how they say a word in order to help others understand their meaning. Is there a way to teach children using PECS to indicate whether they are using a single picture as a request or a comment? How will we interpret a child's meaning if they only give us a single picture? One solution is to teach them to form simple sentences to indicate either "I want ...." or "I see ...."

With our long-term goal in mind, we must introduce a new structure to help children learn to use pictures to express different communicative purposes. Rather than try to teach a child a new structure and a new communicative function at the same time, we prefer to just add one new skill per lesson. Therefore, we will first teach a new language structure (sentence) and then teach a new function (commenting). (See the next chapter for information on teaching commenting.)

We introduce the new structure using the function that the child already knows—requesting. First, we design a sentence strip (see below) that can be readily removed from a communication book and on which we can place pictures to construct a sentence. We design a picture with an icon representing "I want." (We do not use a separate icon for "I" and "want." At this stage, it is not possible to teach what "I" means because the child doesn't have any other pronoun in her picture vocabulary yet to contrast with "I.")

We teach this lesson by starting with the "I want" picture already on the sentence strip, guiding the child to place the picture of what she wants on the sentence strip. The child is then guided to exchange the entire sentence strip. Next, she is taught to place both the "I want" icon and the picture of what is desired onto the sentence strip before giving the strip to someone.

When we are handed the completed sentence strip, we encourage the child to touch each picture while we "read" the sentence to the child (e.g., "I want cookie"). While the child is learning where to place each picture and what to do with the entire sentence strip, we read the sentence strip quickly so as not to delay giving the requested item. Once the sequence has been learned fluently, we begin to introduce a pause between saying, "I want" and the name of the picture of the desired item. This pause tends to encourage children to initially imitate and often say the final spoken word before we do. Although we use this delay strategy to encourage and create opportunities for the child to vocalize, we do not insist on imitation, even for children who are speaking. That is, the expectation is that the child will use PECS, not speak. Several people have reported to us that some children who are pressured to comply with vocal imitation during a PECS exchange begin to avoid using PECS as a way of avoiding the vocal imitation that they find difficult.

Designing Effective Phase 1 and 2 Lessons

Materials needed:

Two or three powerful rewards.

It may help to use rewards that are readily "consumable." For example, snacks, drinks, bubbles, spinning tops, music, or TV (where you control the remote!), etc. If you use toys, books, or other favorite objects, you will need to either have many of them or you will need to get the item back from the child to entice another communicative opportunity.

Pictures, photographs, product logos, or some other type of visual symbol associated with each reward.

The pictures should be sturdy enough to handle frequently. Covering the picture with contact paper or lamination will help preserve the picture. The pictures should be about two inches by two inches. Avoid small pictures (pictures smaller than one inch by one inch) to begin with.

Prerequisites:

The child has been observed to reliably seek out several powerful reinforcers.

People needed:

Two teachers.

One person entices with the reward (and gives the reward when a successful request is made) and the other teacher assists with physical prompting.

Physical arrangement:

Begin with the child in between the two teachers, within arm's length of each teacher. The picture should be placed between the child and the teacher holding the reward.

The child does not have to be seated in a chair. Remember, we arrange this lesson wherever the most powerful rewards are found. Sometimes, that will be on the floor, in the sandbox, in front of the TV, or in some other interesting location. The teacher providing the physical assistance should be behind the child.

Starting the lesson:

Scenario: John and Alexis are Samantha's teachers.

Samantha likes raisins. John will entice Samantha with the raisins, and Alexis will physically help Samantha

pick up, reach, and release the picture into John's hand.
There is a picture of a raisin on the table where Samantha
*is sitting. (Note: It is **not** necessary for Samantha to sit to*
start this lesson—go where the reinforcer is!)

1. At the start of the lesson, John holds up a raisin but
   does not say anything. Samantha sees the raisin
   and reaches for it. John lets Samantha have this
   raisin (using a "first one's free" strategy).
2. After Samantha finishes that raisin, John holds up
   another raisin. Samantha again reaches for it.
   Alexis immediately guides her reaching hand to the
   picture and fully assists in helping her pick it up and
   place it into John's open hand (which John held
   open after he saw Samantha reach for the raisin).
3. As soon as the picture touches John's hand, he
   says, "Raisin!" while immediately giving Samantha
   the raisin.
4. Repeated trials are offered as long as it is apparent
   that Samantha is still motivated to reach for raisins.
   Over these trials, Alexis gradually reduces her
   physical assistance for the release, then the reach,
   and finally for the pick-up. Throughout the trials,
   Alexis says nothing and is not involved in rewarding Samantha for her actions.
5. As Samantha begins to pick up the picture without
   assistance, John and Alexis switch roles. Alexis
   entices with the raisin and Samantha immediately
   gives her the picture.
6. Samantha is now ready for Phase 2 of training.
   Training is now introduced during other highly
   motivating activities for Samantha, such as for her
   favorite toy, a book she likes to look at, her choice
   of drinks (today it's orange juice but tomorrow it
   may be milk!), and related activities. These lessons
   also take place in various parts of the classroom as

well as in different rooms at home. Opportunities to communicate are created throughout the day.

References & Resources

Bondy, A. & Frost, L. (1994). The Picture-Exchange Communication System. *Focus on Autistic Behavior, 9,* 1-19.

Bondy, A. & Frost, L. (in press). The Picture Exchange Communication System. *Behavior Modification.*
This article presents the most recent summary of research regarding PECS and its use.

Bondy, A. & Sulzer-Azaroff, B. (2001). *The Pyramid approach to education in autism, 2ⁿᵈ Edition.* Newark, DE: Pyramid Educational Products, Inc.

Frost, L. & Bondy, A. (1994). *The Picture Exchange Communication System training manual.* Cherry Hill, NJ: PECs, Inc.

Frost, L. & Bondy, A. (2001). *The Picture Exchange Communication System (PECS): 2ⁿᵈ Edition.* Newark, DE: Pyramid Educational Products, Inc.

Frost, L. & Scholefield, D. (May, 1996). Improving picture symbol discrimination skills within PECS through the use of three-dimensional objects and fading: A case study. Paper presented at the Association for Behavior Analysis. San Francisco, CA.

Lovaas, O.I. (1981). *Teaching developmentally disabled children: The me book.* Austin, TX: PRO-ED.

7 | Advanced Lessons within PECS

Kate had learned to request her favorite candy, Skittles, using the sentence strip. Whenever we offered her a handful of Skittles, Kate carefully inspected the choices and selected the red Skittles. If offered other colored Skittles, she pushed them aside. We realized that Kate could select by color even though we had not yet used color within any lesson. The next time she requested a Skittle with her sentence strip, we said "Which one?" We provided a symbol for "red" on her binder and she quickly learned to form the sentence "I want...RED...Skittle." Soon, we were able to find other objects for which color was important to Kate and she used her new attribute whenever it helped clarify what she wanted.

Expanding Sentence Structure

There are two types of extensions to the use of the sentence strip introduced at the end of Chapter 6. One involves expanding on the type of request a child can produce by learning to use attributes such as color, size, shape, etc. The other involves the acquisition of new communication functions (i.e., learning to comment rather than request).

Phase Four (continued): Expanding Requests with Attributes

Once a child has learned how to use the sentence strip to make direct requests, we are able to teach him to clarify what he is requesting. As in the example with Kate, first we noticed that particular colors of candy were important to her, so we taught her how to communicate her preference. We also began to design lessons in which color was made to be important. For example, we placed her favorite toy within a shoebox that had a red cover and placed that box alongside a blue-covered shoebox. To get access to her toy, she needed to request, "I want...RED...box." We designed additional "hiding" games to teach a variety of concepts.

Kris loved chocolate chip cookies and had learned to use a sentence strip to request them. We noticed that if we held a large cookie in one hand and a small piece of cookie in our other hand, Kris invariably reached for the larger piece. In this situation, Kris paid attention to issues related to size—he wanted the big *cookie. We then created a symbol for "big" (i.e., a blob or splotch that fills most of the symbol area) and Kris learned to specify which piece of cookie he preferred.*

In this example, Kris could choose appealing items by their size. However, while it may seem easy to get a child to ask for the larger cookie, how do we teach them to request things that are small? One way is to offer choices in which only the small item fits the situation. For example, if a child could request a spoon to eat pudding out of a small plastic container, giving the child a choice between a regular-sized spoon and the kitchen ladle would increase the appeal of the smaller spoon. Of course, to be certain the child was selecting by the relative size of the spoons, we would later need to offer a choice between the regular spoon and Barbie's spoon! Another approach to this lesson would be to hide a desired item in objects that varied by size. For example, we could put a piece of candy in a small plastic egg while placing tissue paper inside a large plastic egg.

The vocabulary for other attributes, including number, position, placement, and texture, can be introduced within the request function of PECS. (See Table 7-1.) Such lessons tend to be far more motivating to children than lessons involving understanding. Traditionally, attributes (sometimes referred to as "cognitive skills" or "conceptual vocabulary") have been taught to children with autism by placing in front of the student objects varying in the target attribute and telling the child to select by that attribute. For example, we would place a red circle and a blue circle before the child and say, "Touch red. Touch blue," or some similar phrase. When the child correctly responded, we would then praise the child, possibly providing an additional re-

Table 7-1 | Attributes

Type of Attribute	Common Objects with Potential Motivators
Color	Candy, crayons, blocks, Legos, clothes, juice, Skittles, jelly beans
Size a. big v. little b. long v. short	a. Whole cookie vs. crumb, spoons that fit container b. Pretzel rods, string, "Fruit-by-the-Foot," licorice laces
Position	Candy by the chair vs. candy by the table (one he likes, one he dislikes). For example, "I want…cookie…chair" meaning "I want the cookie on the chair, not the one that's on the floor" (where "on" is not providing any critical information).
Shape	Crackers, cookies, cookie cutters, form board puzzles
Relative location	Toy ON the chair vs. toy UNDER the chair (one he likes, one he dislikes). In this case, "on" is providing critical information about which item is desired.
Quantity	10 cookies vs. 1 cookie
Temperature	Cold drink vs. hot drink
Texture	Smooth cloth vs. rough cloth, plain vs. salted pretzel, rough vs. smooth edged potato chips, lumpy vs. smooth cottage cheese
Cleanliness	Clean towel vs. dirty towel
Body parts	Mr. Potato Head, placement of Band-Aids, or lotion
Action words	"hit," "bounce," "throw," "catch" the ball

ward. Using the request function within PECS involves items that clearly are important to the child. The reward for successful requests is receiving the item the child specified.

Designing Effective Lessons Involving Attributes

Materials needed:

Items that vary only along the dimension associated with the attribute to be taught. (See the table on the previous page for examples of attributes and potential common objects.)

Prerequisites:

Before teaching a particular attribute within PECS, be sure that the child shows a preference associated with that attribute in terms of real items (not necessarily communicatively). For example, a child who selectively picks out red candies to eat, the blue crayon to draw with, or the white paper to draw on is demonstrating actions governed by color as an attribute dimension. In such cases, it will be very motivating to the child using PECS to request items with that specific feature.

It is very important to understand that a child can "know" or "respond to" an attribute without being able to communicate about the attribute or understand our attempt to communicate about that attribute. For example, I have met many teachers who were convinced that their student could not master "big" vs. "little." These teachers had done hours and hours worth of drills on "touch big" and "touch little" with various sized circles or squares, to no avail. However, with these same students, if I approached with a whole (big) cookie in one hand and a cookie crumb (little) in my other hand, I noticed that these students reliably took the big cookie and did not randomly respond (as long as they liked cookies!). The trick may be to separate the visual skill (or the skill associated with other senses such as touch, hearing, etc.) from the communicative skill associated with that sensory property.

If the child does not show a "natural" inclination to select by color, it may be possible to test the ability to visually discriminate a type of attribute without requiring communicative understanding. For example, assume that Katie likes cookies. While she is watching, put a cookie inside an open white-sided shoebox. You do not need to say, "Where is the cookie? Find the cookie. Look inside the box" or anything else. Just show

her where you are placing the cookie. If she reliably reaches inside the box to take the cookie, then, over several trials, gradually place the lid on the shoebox. When you show her that you placed the cookie inside the shoebox and put the lid on top of the box, if she reliably opens the box to get her cookie, you are ready to move to the next step. Now, you will want to have two shoeboxes: one with a red lid and the other with a blue lid. Show Katie that the cookie is placed inside a box and place the red lid over that box and the blue lid over the empty box. Over trials, sometimes cover the cookie with the red lid and sometimes cover it with the blue lid, and be sure to move around the position of the lids. If Katie reliably finds her cookie, then she is showing us she "knows" color. Next, we want to teach her to communicate about color.

When using an attribute such as color, try to avoid using a symbol with a perfect circle filled with that color. In such cases, the child may be confused as to whether he should pay attention to the color or the shape of the color.

People needed:

One teacher can effectively teach this lesson.

Physical arrangement:

Have several pairs of items that vary only in the one attribute you are teaching.

For example, if you are focusing on color, you will need pairs of items that are identical except for their color—candy, toy cars, crayons, etc. Although this step will involve more time in preparation, it will ultimately pay off in reducing how long you will spend on teaching this lesson.

Starting the lesson:

Scenario: Debbie is Rob's mom.

Rob likes Skittles (small fruit-flavored candies with brightly colored coatings). Whenever Debbie offers Rob a handful of Skittles, Rob very carefully takes the red ones. Debbie will use this preference to design the lesson. (Note: It is **not** necessary for Rob to have learned to follow commands involving the word "red" ("Touch red") or for him to have mastered matching-to-sample with colors to begin this lesson. All that is necessary is for Rob to be able to communicate his desire for Skittles using sentence structure (Phase IV in PECS) and his demonstrated preference for the red ones.)

1. Rob approaches Debbie with a sentence strip containing "I want....Skittle." Debbie shows Rob two Skittles, one red and one blue. Rob reaches for the red Skittle.

2. Debbie pulls back the Skittles (and she may shrug her shoulders, or say, "Which one?) and manually guides Rob to pick up a symbol for "red" on the front of the communication book. (Note that it is the physical guidance more than a spoken question that helps teach Rob what to do in this situation.) Debbie helps Rob place that symbol on the sentence strip between "I want" and "Skittle."

3. As Rob hands over the sentence strip, Debbie takes it, helps Rob touch each picture in order, while saying, "I want RED Skittle." Debbie immediately gives Rob the red Skittle. Of course, she does not try to make Rob say "red" or any other word.

4. Over the next several minutes, Debbie continues to entice Rob with Skittles and gradually reduces her manual assistance to guide Rob to use the "red" symbol within his sentence strip.

5. At other times, Debbie notices that Rob has his own way of building a stack of blocks. He seems to know precisely which block he wants next. Debbie holds onto a red block just as Rob is reaching for it. In

this manner, Rob is encouraged to put together "I
want...red...block" on his sentence strip.

6. Debbie continues to find situations in which Rob
   seems to have clear color choices and gradually
   introduces other color symbols into the communication system.

7. Finally, Debbie occasionally checks for correspondence with Rob. When Rob asks for a red crayon,
   Debbie holds up several crayons and simply says,
   "Go ahead, take it." If Rob takes the red crayon,
   then Debbie has another indication of Rob's level of
   skill regarding communicating about colors.

Phase Five: Teaching Answering Simple Questions

If your training in PECS has gone well up to this point of the
training sequence, your child should be able to request spontaneously, using sentence structure and possibly attributes. In order
to teach the more advanced skill of commenting, you will need to
be able to ask your child simple questions about objects and events
in the surroundings.

Since the PECS method teaches only one new skill at a time,
you will need to introduce simple questions with the current communicative function used by your child, namely, requesting. At
this point in the training sequence, your child has not heard the
question, "What do you want?" Therefore, learning to respond to
this question is our next step.

Teaching a child who can spontaneously request with a
sentence strip is relatively easy. We simply need to ask the question "What do you want?" prior to presenting him with something desired. Over time, we could eliminate presenting items
and solely ask the question. When we begin this lesson, it also is
helpful to point to the "I want" representation while asking,
"What do you want?" As quickly as possible over a series of

opportunities, we would gradually introduce and increase a delay between asking our question and pointing to "I want." In time, children come to respond to the question before the teacher points to the "I want" icon. Pairing your question with pointing to one picture in this lesson will prepare your child for the use of this strategy in our next lesson.

A word of caution is appropriate at this point. We have found that once teachers and parents can rely on the child's ability to respond to "What do you want?" they often abandon their previous emphasis on spontaneity. Therefore, to preserve a blend of spontaneity and responding to questioning by others, you must plan to provide a minimum number of opportunities for spontaneous requesting each day. You should expect at least five spontaneous requests per day without setting a minimum number of answers.

Phase Six: Teaching Commenting

Once a child has learned to reply to "What do you want?" we are ready to teach responding to other simple questions, such as, "What do you see? What do you hear? What do you have?" To effectively teach these lessons, we must remember two points. First, we must remember that comments result in social consequences, not receiving the noted item. If we say, "What do you see?" and the child responds, "I see...spoon" we would respond, "Yes! It is a spoon! I see the spoon, too!" We would *not* give the child the spoon. If we did that, then the child would learn that this phrase is just another way to ask for something, such as "I'd like the spoon" or "Give me the spoon."

Second, we must understand the types of things and events that lead typically developing children to comment. Very young children do not comment about static aspects of their environment—they do not initially say, "I see the floor....I see the wall...." Instead, they first comment about things that change or are out of the ordinary. For example, they comment about the dog walking into the room, about the milk that just spilt, about a toy that is out of place, etc. Therefore, to design effective commenting lessons, we should strive to use similar types of interesting and eye-catching (or the equivalent of ear-catching, etc.) aspects of their surroundings. The more appealing the item used in the lesson, the more likely the child will notice that item.

We begin this lesson by suddenly changing something, such as taking a toy out of a box. As we take the item out, we ask, "Oh! What do you see?" or "Look! What is it?" While we ask our question, we point to an icon representing "I see" that has been placed on the communication book (on the left side on the cover of the communication binder). The child is likely to pick up the picture pointed to because that was a skill acquired in previous lessons. (Note: It may help to have only the "I see" icon on the cover for these initial commenting trials. Later, the child will learn to choose between "I want" and "I see.") The child may next place the appropriate picture on the sentence strip and hand it to the teacher. As before, the teacher reads the full sentence back to the child and enthusiastically praises him!

It may be very helpful to select items that are interesting but not your child's all-time favorites. A child who has become used to receiving something concrete when he uses PECS may be surprised (if not shocked!) when nothing concrete is forthcoming. This reaction would be more dramatic for items that were highly desired.

As your child learns this lesson, it is important to assure that he has opportunities to request, both spontaneously and in response to direct questions. Therefore, your child will need to distinguish between the questions, "What do you want?" and "What do you see?" and their corresponding icons.

At this point, you must make one more change in your teaching strategy to promote spontaneous commenting. Essentially, you must eliminate your questions so that only the change or interesting aspect in the environment triggers a comment from your child. You may gradually eliminate the question, by leaving off the end of the question. For example, you could say, "Look! What do….?" gradually eliminating all words within your question. Finally, if you had been using exclamatory expressions such as "Look! Wow! Oh!" preceding your direct question, then you could eliminate the question, leaving just the exclamation. Over time, you would then eliminate your expression as well.

What Comes After Phase Six?

Children who have completed each of the phases of PECS described in this book will be able to request wanted and needed items spontaneously and in response to questions, comment about aspects of their world, again both spontaneously and in answer to questions, and accomplish each function using various attributes and adjectives.

Of course, there are other aspects to language development that need to be acquired. Some of these, including social greetings, answering "yes" vs. "no," and requesting help, may involve some gestural skills as previously noted. There is nothing incompatible about teaching these simple gestures while also teaching a child to use PECS. One emphasis is to teach with strategies that promote spontaneity rather than rely solely on imitation. For example, a child needs to ask for help before he has a tantrum over some frustrating circumstance. The teaching strategies for initiating asking for help or a break may require the same type of two-person teaching strategy used during the initial aspect of teaching PECS. (See the example at the end of Chapter 4.)

The teaching strategies and sequence of skill acquisition outlined for PECS also may be beneficial when teaching language skills with other modalities. That is, the techniques and decisions described for PECS—early focus on requesting, two-person prompting, delayed prompting, shaping, fading, formal error-correction, etc.—are not limited to using picture systems to communicate. These strategies can readily be incorporated into other types of communication systems, especially using two trainers to promote initiation.

Using PECS at School and at Home

The key to the success of PECS, or any other communication system, is for it to be used as often as possible. For this system to be effective, it cannot be scheduled for use "from 10:00 AM to 10:15 AM and from 2:00 PM to 2:15 PM," nor simply during snack time. This system must be viewed as the child's communication system, something that is potentially helpful in all situations. Limiting its use or limiting access to the communication book to times when adults are ready to use it does not promote the development of spontaneous, functional communication.

Children who speak can do so at any time and in any situation. Therefore, you must assure that your child has access to his communication book at all times, although the vocabulary used at home may differ from that used at school. We see using PECS at home (if initially taught at school) as part of the second phase of training. You also should encourage your child to use the system with everyone in the home, not just you, the parents.

At School

When can children use PECS at school? We suggest that the school team (including the teacher, assistants, and the speech-language pathologist, and the parents at home) analyze all activities, noting the materials associated with each activity. For example, the art activity may involve paper, scissors, and crayons, while the circle time activity involves puppets associated with songs and sunny vs. cloudy pictures associated with the weather. Each of the materials is a potential source of communication.

Once your child has learned the routine associated with a particular activity, the teacher can interrupt or undermine the activity by removing a necessary item (Sulzer-Azaroff & Mayer, 1994). For example, your child may have learned to wash his hands and then use a towel to dry them. If we remove the towel one day, we have created a situation that promotes asking for the missing towel to complete the sequence. In the second phase of training, your child's school team should seek to find many such communicative opportunities throughout the teaching day as a way of expanding the use of PECS. (More details on this strategy are reviewed in the next chapter.) In addition, it is important that school staff encourage your child to use PECS to communicate with peers, as described in the section below.

At Home

At home, we suggest a similar tactic. That is, consider the many natural routines that occur in a home environment, routines that will become part of the rest of your child's life. Examples include setting the table and routines associated with meal preparation and clean up. If your child has been taught to routinely set the table, then a communicative opportunity can be created by sabotaging the routine (with appropriate adjustments for the age of your child). For instance, you could remove all the forks from the drawer where they are usually kept. Some routines are uniquely related to the home situation and may be difficult to replicate at school. Examples of home-based routines include:

1. Cleaning, folding, and putting away clothes (the latter can be viewed as a sorting or categorization task). For example, within these routines, a child can learn to request missing items.

2. Washing, showering, or bathing and associated objects (soap, towels, etc.) and toys (for the bath tub). For example, a child can learn to request needed items (e.g., soap) vs. desired items (e.g., the rubber ducky).
3. Unloading and sorting groceries (food or household supplies). In these situations, the child can learn to follow a schedule or to request necessary materials.
4. Cleaning and straightening the house.

Of course, we must keep age-appropriate goals in mind. For a three-year-old, cleaning may involve tidying up his toys, folding clothes may involve folding socks in half, setting the table may involve placing paper cups on each placemat, etc.

Each family may have their own special routines. We strongly recommend teaching and expecting children to participate in such routines. The following chart may be helpful in identifying potential vocabulary within common routines (feel free to add your own!):

Table 7-2 | Finding Vocabulary within Routines

Routine	Area of House	Vocabulary
Making cereal	Kitchen	Cereal, bowl, spoon, milk, sugar
Bath time	Bathroom	Bubble bath, washcloth, sponge, boats, bathtub stickers, toy duck
Going outside to play	House, then backyard	Shoes, coat, hat, swing, ball, slide
Bedtime	Bedroom	Pillow, favorite blanket, book or specific books

Watching your child's preferences in the home is also crucial to developing increased communication. Some children enjoy watching TV or their favorite videotapes, while other children have favorite songs. Some children have favorite toys or other household objects, while other children enjoy playing in the basement or the backyard. Your child can learn to request all of these activities spontaneously, and, as he acquires sentence structure, to clarify his requests with attributes and adjectives.

Using PECS with Peers and Siblings

I observed Jane, a child with autism and skilled in PECS, who had been placed in a preschool class with typically developing children. As I observed, a small group of children, including Jane, was playing appropriately with small, plastic figures. At first it was difficult to distinguish Jane from her peers. Then, the other children became interested in toys in another area of the room and left as a group—except for Jane. She continued to play as before. One of the children from the group came back to encourage her to join them. Jane continued to play as before.

As I continued to observe Jane, it became clear that, although she had some skills in playing with toys in an appropriate manner, she did not initiate, respond to, or maintain social interactions with the other children. If an adult in the class held a figurine that she wanted, she immediately went to her communication book, constructed a complete sentence, and exchanged her request for the item. She was never observed to initiate communication or social interaction with her peers. I wondered how we would change this pattern.

So far, this book has focused on teaching the child with autism to use PECS with adults. We began by teaching PECS use with adults because it is typically adults who control access to the significant desires of a child. Adults generally control access to drinks and snacks, playthings, TV or the video, and visits to various places outside the class and home. It is not unusual to see children with autism acquire good communication skills with PECS (or speech or any other communication modality, for that matter) but limit its use to adults. How do we teach children like Jane to communicate with their peers and siblings?

We know we must encourage contact between our children and their peers. However, we also know that mere exposure is not sufficient to result in significant improvements in communication or play with peers. We often have seen a communication progression involving peers that parallels the sequence observed in learning to communicate with adults. That is, children accustomed to using PECS with adults will initially do so with children to the extent that these other children have things that are of interest.

Educators at the University of Washington developed a strategy that capitalizes on the tendency of children with autism to pursue things of interest to them (Schwartz, Garfinkle, & Bauer, 1998). They were aware that adults tend to control the distribution of drinks and edible treats at snack time. In their integrated preschool, they decided to give some of the snacks to the peers of several children who knew how to use PECS. At first, some of the children with autism made their request to their teachers, but these were ignored. Most children quickly noticed that a peer now held their favorite snack. While some children needed some teacher assistance, others used PECS spontaneously with peers. Now came the tricky part—the peers had to be willing to share! This was encouraged by the teachers and richly praised when accomplished. Soon, the children with autism were using PECS to communicate with adults and peers.

These educational researchers also observed communication in other situations in which the teachers did not specifically encourage the use of PECS. They found that the children who had learned to communicate with peers during snack time also communicated with them in these novel situations. Furthermore, the researchers also observed increased social approach and interaction (i.e., both initiating and responding to peers) in novel situations that did not involve any formal communication.

From this work and our own experience, it now seems relatively easy to teach children using PECS to communicate with their peers and siblings. The keys are three-fold:

1. Distribute desired or needed objects to peers and siblings. For example, during an art activity, have someone other than the teacher be responsible for distributing the crayons, paper, and other necessary materials.

2. Make sure that peers and siblings understand the content of the pictures and symbols used by the child using PECS. While very young children may not be able to respond successfully to PECS, we have observed effective interactions with children as young as two years old.

3. Peers and siblings need to respond to PECS just as they would to speech. That is, they should be encouraged and supported for sharing what was requested. Of course, with young children, it may be easier to teach them to "share" things they are not thrilled with. For example, if Mary doesn't really like popcorn, she is more likely to give some to Bill than if he asked her for her favorite cookie. (Note: In the next chapter, we will discuss additional strategies that help peers better communicate with children using PECS or other communication modalities.)

Can children using PECS use their communication skills with other children with disabilities? As long as we have kept the three issues noted above in mind, we have seen successful use of PECS within groups of children with various disabilities, including autism.

What Is the Relationship between PECS and Speech Development?

Although this book is written primarily for an audience interested in individuals who do not speak, many members of that audience undoubtedly hope that these individuals will learn to speak. A reasonable concern is: will using an alternative communication system such as PECS interfere with or inhibit the potential acquisition of speech? As discussed in Chapter 5, there is no empirical, published evidence that introducing such a system will inhibit the development of speech. In fact, information that we have gathered regarding young children who learned PECS strongly suggests that the opposite happens. That is, use of PECS for more than one year by children with autism younger than six years is strongly associated with the acquisition of speech.

In 1994, we reviewed the communication modality for a number of children with autism who received educational services in a statewide public school program (Bondy and Frost, 1994a). The program provided full-day, year-round services, had a high staff-to-child ratio, and provided highly structured, behaviorally oriented services, including the use of PECS when appropriate. We tracked the communicative progress of nineteen children who began using PECS before the age of six years but who had used the system for less than one year at the time of the assessment. Of these students, only two had acquired independent speech, and five were using speech primarily while they were using PECS. The other twelve students relied solely on PECS to functionally communicate. At the same time, we reviewed a group of sixty-six children who had started using PECS at the same age as the other group but who had used the system for more than one year. Of this group, forty-one demonstrated independent speech and another twenty used speech in conjunction with PECS.

Several points of caution should be made about this information. First, this information was retrospectively collected. That is, we had not randomly assigned students to receive PECS training or not. Thus, we have not demonstrated that learning PECS causes children to acquire speech. Furthermore, when we describe a child as having "independent speech" we mean that speech was the child's sole means of communication, not that the child had necessarily acquired age-appropriate language skills. Thus, while some children who had used PECS developed age-appropriate spoken language, others acquired a much more limited ability to use language. Still, our retrospective analysis not only suggests that the use of PECS did not inhibit the development of speech in this group of children but also may have contributed to its development.

A related question that often occurs following the introduction of PECS is how to respond to a child who may begin to speak after months or even years of silently using PECS? On hearing those first spoken words, both parents and professionals have the tendency to put the PECS book away and insist that the child only use speech to communicate. Our experience in such situations suggests a more cautious and gradual approach is best for reasons illustrated in the following two examples.

Ernie was introduced to PECS when he was just about three years old. At the time, he rarely made any sounds. He quickly acquired the early skills associated with PECS. When he began to use the sentence strip, his teachers began to use the delayed read-back strategy. (That is, they paused between reading back "I want" and the next picture on the sentence strip, hoping to encourage him to fill in what he wanted.) Ernie then began to approximate some of the words in the sentence. During the next several months, his sentence structure became more complex and his ability to vocally imitate improved. Soon, his exchange of the sentence strip reliably led to his saying each word that corresponded with the pictures. Over the next few months, he occasionally would construct a sentence and then say the sentence without giving the strip to the teacher. He also began to say some words and simple phrases without using his communication book. Approximately twenty-four months after the introduction of PECS, he ceased using the system and used speech for all of his communication skills.

In Figure 7-1 you can follow Ernie's sequence of picture and spoken-word usage after his introduction to PECS. He acquired his first PECS symbols during the first day of training. He rapidly progressed in acquiring additional pictures as he moved through the phases of training. We heard his first reliable speech-sounds after six months, but his first reliable word was not spoken until about twelve months after he entered the program.

Figure 7-1

Note that after Ernie's first words were spoken, he did begin to speak more and more. At the same time, his picture vocabulary also increased (by fifty percent in the four months after his first word). This growth involved new vocabulary, new syntax, and new communicative functions. We were able to use Ernie's more advanced skills with PECS to help him improve his speech skills. For example, near the end of using PECS, Ernie displayed some difficulty adding "-ing" to certain verbs (e.g., "He is walking"). When an icon for "-ing" was added to his communication book, and he was taught to construct sentences with this icon, his speech production began to include the appropriate verb ending. What would have happened if we had pulled his communication book away at the point when his first words appeared? At that point, he could only say or imitate single words, but he could construct multi-element sentences with visual symbols.

Here is another example that illustrates why it pays not to be too hasty in weaning children from PECS once they have begun to speak. For several children who were using speech while continuing to use PECS, we set up comparable situations with and without access to their communication books (Frost, Daly, & Bondy, 1997). Although these children used some limited speech when their communication systems were not available, their speech was significantly more sophisticated and comprehensive when their PECS books were accessible. For example, one child would say "cookie" or occasionally "I want" without PECS, but with her system, she put together a complete sentence strip and then said, "I want two green toys" or "I want big yellow candy." If we were to take this child's PECS book away or try to force her to communicate only via speech, she could not communicate as well as she could using her visual communication system.

From our perspective, if someone were to suddenly take away a child's communication binder in an attempt to promote more speech, the resultant loss of skills (even in hopes of their replacement in the future) would be unethical. During a transition from one system to another, no skills should be lost. We should preserve a child's skill not only in terms of the total number of pictures (words) used, but also in terms of the complexity of the sentences the child can construct. We would also want to assure that if the child spoke, at least seventy percent of his words could be understood by a stranger before a visual back-up communication system was removed.

Finally, remember that PECS is used to teach functional communication, not to teach speech. Of course, it is delightful when children do acquire speech and such changes should receive lots of reinforcement! For those children who continue to use PECS and whose vocabulary continues to grow (over 120 or so pictures), switching to an electronic system may help promote continued vocabulary growth and ease picture selection. (Refer back to Chapter 5 for information on AAC strategies.)

Troubleshooting with PECS and Where to Go for Help

The table on the next page provides a listing of the most frequent mistakes that teachers and parents make when implementing PECS. The table describes the most common mistakes within each phase and suggests straightforward solutions to these problems.

How to Say "NO!" and Live to Tell about It

As soon as a child starts making effective requests, we adults face a complex choice. Should we always give the child what he requests?

Early in training of PECS or any other communication system, the initial requests are very important and everyone wants to be sure to reward those requests. Thus, if a boy asks for 100 pieces of pretzel on the first day of training, I am very likely to give him 100 (very small!) pieces of pretzel, as I am so excited with his new skill. However, after several days, I am not as ex-

Table 7-3 | Most Frequent Mistakes in Each Phase of PECS

Phase	Most Common Mistake	Potential Solution
I. Initiation	1. No reinforcer 2. Verbal prompting (e.g., "What do you want?" "Give me the picture." 3. Physical prompting before reach	1. Find powerful reward 2. Practice silence 3. Wait for the reach
II. Persistence	1. One trainer 2. Only used at snack-time	1. Wait for 2nd trainer 2. Create rewarding situations all day long
III. Choice making	1. Waiting too long to start (e.g., acquiring 50 pictures before starting this phase) 2. Starting with many rewards (e.g., everything at snack time) 3. Waiting to reward until child gives the picture 4. Insisting on one type of symbol (e.g., all pictures *must* be black-and-white)	1. Start when 6 to 12 rewards are used 2. Start with one preferred and one non-preferred 3. Give feedback on choice of symbol 4. Be flexible and try other strategies or symbols

cited to give him what he asks for every single time he asks. So, what are my choices? We've held off on this question until now because the full range of responses available to me depends on many lessons. Here are some options:

1. If the boy has eaten all the pretzels, show him the empty bag and don't say "no." Let him get angry at

Phase	Most Common Mistake	Potential Solution
IVa. Sentence structure	1. Waiting too long to start this phase 2. Verbally prompting 3. Insisting on speech	1. You don't have to complete III to start IV 2. Not yet! Use physical prompts 3. Not now—not ever!
IVb. Attributes	1. Using only one attribute with one object 2. Insisting child complete matching-to-sample before starting this phase	1. Teach many qualifiers—color, shape, size, etc. 2. Start when the attribute is important to the child
V. Answering questions	1. Eliminating initiation (e.g., asking "What do you want?" at every opportunity and thus undermining spontaneity)	1. Create opportunities to respond and initiate
VI. Commenting	1. Boring materials 2. Predictable repetition	1. Materials should attract attention 2. Use surprise and change
Transition from PECS to Speech	1. Insisting on speech imitation 2. Taking the pictures/PECS away from child 3. Rewarding only speech	1. Reward all successful functional communication 2. Let child set the pace 3. Bigger reward for speech

the bag rather than you! Quickly offer him some alternatives. In this situation, he is likely to see the futility of asking for more pretzels.

2. If it is simply not time for pretzels (or whatever his requested item or activity), then take the pretzel

picture and put it on the schedule indicating when it will be time to have a snack.

3. Give him a "wait" card (see Chapter 8) and during the wait time, entice him with alternatives that are available. At the end of the wait, see if he'll choose another item.

4. Show him a card with the available reinforcer menu and suggest he can choose from the menu. Essentially, this strategy is similar to what would happen if an adult walked into a 7-Eleven™ store and requested caviar. He'd be politely informed that he can order a can of tuna fish but no caviar will be forthcoming—no matter how often he asks!

5. If you have no available menu, you may want to place a universal NO (Ø) sign on the pretzel card, or place the card on a board with a red vs. green side. The items on the green side are available, while those on the red side are not.

6. Consider whether it is worthwhile to negotiate with the child. Perhaps if he did something terrific (learned a new skill, cleaned up his room, etc.), you would be willing to make a deal with him. In this case, use his request to start the token system described in the next chapter.

7. In the end, you may simply have to say "no" and then accept as you watch the child have a tantrum. Of course, do make sure the child does not get hurt (or hurt others). Do not give in to the child at this point, or tantrums will become (or stay) the primary mode of requesting. While the child is crying or otherwise being upset, show the child—possibly with other children—what other rewards are available, and see if you can entice a different request.

Of course, the choice that many will want to take—simply take the pretzel picture away from the child—is what you should absolutely never do! These are the child's pictures, part of his communication system. They are *not* the teacher's or parent's pictures. Do speaking children ever nag us with their persistent requests and questions? Of course. While we might think of taping their mouths shut, we never do. And we similarly never take away the child's ability to communicate with us. We may not agree to or reward every request a child makes, but that is a natural part of growing up in any society.

Where to Go for Help

Hopefully, the suggestions above will help prevent problems or help you design successful modifications. Of course, you may run into unanticipated problems or simply have questions about how to apply the PECS system to your child. In such cases, there are several ways you may precede.

First, it is important to have a member of your team who is competent in applied behavior analysis. The strategies described here have all been developed within this field, which focuses on the science of learning, and, thus, teaching. For guidelines regarding identifying and evaluating the skills such a specialist should have, contact the Association for Behavior Analysis, listed in the Resource Guide at the end of this book. The Autism Special Interest Group of this organization has written a set of guidelines that can help parents and others to identify skilled professionals in this field (*Guidelines for Consumers of Applied Behavior Analysis Services to Individuals with Autism*).

Second, a competent speech-language pathologist should also be an important team member. He or she can evaluate your child's communication abilities, both formally, with tests, and informally through observation; provide input about AAC methods; and advise parents and school staff about ways to incorporate language learning into your child's daily routine. In this area, the American Speech-Language Hearing Association can supply appropriate guidelines regarding competency.

For additional guidance on the phases and associated teaching strategies of PECS, you can refer to our manual, *The Picture Exchange Communication System Training Manual*, 2nd Edition, Frost and Bondy (2001). There also is a videotape that provides a more visual overview regarding the system. These materials, as well as contact information for helpful organizations, are listed in the Resource Guide.

References & Resources

Schwartz, I., Garfinkle, A. & Bauer, J. (1998). The Picture Exchange Communication System: Communicative outcomes for young children with disabilities. *Topics in Early Childhood Special Education,* 10-15.

Frost, L., Daly, M. & Bondy, A. (April, 1997). Speech features with and without access to PECS for children with autism. Paper presented at COSAC. Long Beach, NJ.

Weiss, M.J. & Harris, S. L. (2001). *Reaching out, joining in: Teaching social skills to young children with autism.* Bethesda: Woodbine House.

8 | Using Visual Strategies to Enhance Understanding

I worked with a teenager named Enrico. He never spoke but effectively used PECS to request his favorite things. At times, Enrico would become extremely agitated and begin to smack his head with his hand. If you stood too close to him when he was agitated, he would try to smack you. We wondered whether he simply didn't want to do what we asked or whether he didn't always understand what was said to him. We arranged to give Enrico a set of simple spoken instructions about common items in the classroom. He retrieved only one of ten items and engaged in head slapping following almost every instruction. We then used pictures to instruct him about the same set of items. When we used pictures, not only did he retrieve all the items but he also did not hit his head during any instruction. Clearly, this pattern was more consistent with a comprehension problem than a compliance problem.

The emphasis of the previous chapters has been on systems designed to help children and adults improve their ability to communicate with us. That is, they have been concerned with improving *expressive* language skills. In this chapter, we will focus on ways of using visual systems to help these individuals better understand our attempts to communicate—in other words, to improve their *receptive* language skills.

Understanding Instructions

A fundamental skill is to understand simple instructions, such as requests to get a common item, go to a location, or answer a direct question. In Chapter 2, we pointed out the importance of understanding not only things said to us but also of understanding various visual symbols. As in our example with Enrico, we also must remember that some individuals respond better to visual cues than to auditory cues. (A more complete description of this type of situation is presented in a study by Peterson, Bondy, Vincent, and Finnegan, 1996.)

We all respond to many visual cues in our surroundings:

1. **Personal**—day timers, calendars, clocks, Post-it notes, notes to ourselves, shopping lists, pagers;
2. **Public**—road signs (including words, arrows, sign-post shapes and colors), restroom symbols, emergency signs, lines painted on the road, advertisements on public transportation, route numbers on busses or trains.

From this list we can see that there are many visual symbols that we all must learn to understand to function effectively in our society. We believe it is important to teach children and adults who do not speak to understand visual symbols as well. Traditionally, this type of lesson has been taught using a strategy called "matching-to-sample."

Many different materials and objects can be used during a matching lesson, but one goal is for children to select an item when we show them a representation of that item. For example, if I hold up a picture of a ball and the child gets a real ball, but when I show a picture of a cup the child gets a real cup, then we conclude that the child understands what the pictures mean. Many teachers have simplified this type of lesson by having the child point to the corresponding item. In this case, we might have various objects on a tabletop and then show the child a series of pictures. If the child reliably touches the items that correspond to the pictures, then we would say she has learned this task.

In addition to showing students pictures and expecting them to point to the corresponding items, we can also reverse the direction of this lesson. That is, we can hold up various objects and teach the child to point to the corresponding picture. There is a fascinating field within behavior analysis (called *stimulus equivalence*) that has shown that learning this lesson in one direction (i.e., object to picture) actually helps the child understand the lesson in the other direction (i.e., picture to object).

The question that can be raised about such lessons is whether they can be viewed as communicative. Such lessons are led by the teacher (the teacher holds up the initial object and the child points to the corresponding picture) and the response by the child is directed to the picture, not necessarily the teacher. This is why we suggest that such lessons should be part of a total educational package, but should not be viewed as a prerequisite to beginning lessons involving functional communication. In fact, if you introduce PECS to a child *before* you try to teach her picture-to-object lessons, such lessons may never be necessary. In other words, the child may learn picture-to-object correspondence in the course of learning to communicate with PECS.

Teaching Instruction Following

Throughout this book, our emphasis has been on teaching communication in a manner that is functional to the child—through lessons that involve objects and activities that are important and immediately a part of the child's everyday life. We need to continue this emphasis when teaching children to understand language.

Recall that one reason we learn to understand other people is that they often have information that is important to us. If we arrange these "listening" lessons so that the child learns the importance of understanding what we are trying to communicate, we can enhance the lesson's effectiveness. For example, you could try to teach your child to go to the couch, chair, or door on command. If she went where you requested, you might praise her. If your child did not like and anticipate praise as a response, she likely wouldn't respond to many of these directions in the future. To make this lesson functional, you could hide something important to your child (candy, a toy, etc.) on or near a particular item. For example, if your child used PECS to indicate she wanted candy, you could respond by communicating (in a simple manner) that the candy was on the couch. When your child got to the couch, she would find the candy and thus be rewarded for having understood the direction.

A related approach is to have your child experience a pleasant, natural consequence when she goes to the couch, chair, or door when instructed. For example, the natural consequence of going to a door is getting to go outside, the consequence of going to a couch to sit is getting to watch TV, etc. When using this strategy, it is important to tie the natural consequence in to following the instruction.

When we begin to teach a child to understand the picture or symbol we will use within this instruction-following routine, it is important to make sure that the child understands the picture by itself. That is, while there may be times when we want to combine speech with visual cues, if a child responded to the combination, then we would not know for certain whether she reacted to the spoken words alone, the picture alone, or needed the combination of both for understanding. Given the need in our society to respond to visual cues in isolation from auditory cues, this lesson is important for all students. Thus, we suggest teaching the instructional use of visual cues without accompanying speech.

To start this type of lesson, we first make sure that the object to be used in teaching the child to follow instructions is very familiar to her. The item should either be one that the child enjoys (like a ball) or that she knows what to do with (e.g., put plates on the table before a meal). For example, just before breakfast, we might use a picture of a bowl to signal to the child to get her bowl so we can serve breakfast. This picture would be a good choice only if the child has experienced that when bowls are on the table in the morning, cereal is about to be served! We would show the child a picture of the bowl and then quietly guide her to where the bowls are kept. The first few times we did this lesson, we would walk the child completely through the routine so there are no mistakes. Over time, we would start the lesson in the same manner, but then begin to let the child complete small portions of the end of the sequence. We would gradually reduce our help so that we would only need to show her the picture and she would get the bowl and put it on the table and await her cereal.

At other times of the day, we would go through this same teaching strategy with other important materials (e.g., a ball to take to gym, a crayon to take to the art area, a book to join morning circle, etc.). In this manner, we would try to build a set of pictures and/or visual symbols that the child associates with using materials in an understandable manner. We might also want to teach the child to respond to pictures or other visual cues that can be associated with specific areas (e.g., the art table) or activities (e.g., morning circle). To teach her to understand spoken instructions, we could pair them either with the effective pictures or the functional items themselves.

Finally, we should consider whether our goal is to teach *instruction following,* where the focus is on understanding the instruction, or *compliance training,* where the focus is on doing what we say (whether it fits the situation or not). For example, if we want to teach Mary to understand the instruction, "Go to the door," then we would be certain that something related to "doors" happens when she gets to the door (e.g., she gets to go outside). In similar fashion, instructions about the sink, refrigerator, a ball, etc. would all be connected with appropriate activities. On the other hand, if our point is to teach Mary to do what we say for the sake of compliance, then we could say, "Go to the door" and praise her when she gets there (but not have her go outside).

Although there are times when compliance for its own sake is important, it is not necessary to begin all instruction-following lessons with compliance as the focus. Furthermore, many young children with autism do not respond well to the social praise used in teaching compliance. In fact, some may learn to comply simply to avoid the physical prompts used when they do not do as they are asked.

Types of Symbols to Use

We've noted the importance of teaching all children to understand not only our spoken words, but also to understand various visual signals. What symbols should we select? If your child is using PECS, a good idea is to use the same type of symbols she is accustomed to within PECS. However, to avoid confusion, it may be helpful to use pictures your child is able to understand but that are much larger than the ones used within the communication book (for example, four-inch squares instead of two-inch squares). That is, your child gives two-inch square pictures to request items but is given four-inch square pictures by parents and teachers as part of an instructional interaction.

If your child is not using PECS, you may want to use any symbol that the child can understand—that is, photographs, product logos, miniature or full-sized items, three-dimensional representations, and similar symbols.

Schedule Following

Most adults, especially those living hectic lives, use some sort of calendar system to keep track of important appointments and errands. We do this even if we have very good verbal skills. That is, even though I could probably make myself memorize all of the things I am supposed to do, I have learned that I act much more responsibly when I use various visual cues to help me remember what I am expected to accomplish.

One of our teaching values is to teach children things that we have found to be important in our own lives. That is, if it's good for us, it's most likely good for the kids. Therefore, since we use a calendar system to help remind us about what is going to happen in our lives, we believe it is a good idea to teach children to use a similar system. Some children with autism may have fewer tantrums and other outbursts once they better understand the expectations for their time at school or at home.

Teaching children and adults to follow a schedule is similar to teaching them to follow visual instructions. In fact, we prefer to start teaching children to follow a schedule after they have learned to respond to individual pictures. A schedule is a sequence of pictures or other symbols. What is important here is to teach your child to use the sequence of symbols rather than depending on a teacher or parent to tell her what to do. So, one simple rule is to avoid saying, "Go check your schedule." If you're willing to say that to your child, you may as well tell her what to do! Instead, teach your child to respond to natural cues in the environment, including:

1. Finishing a task (by running out of materials or using all materials);
2. Sounds that signal the end of activities, either environmental (a bell, chime, alarms, etc.) or from people (the teacher says, "Music is over!");
3. Visual signals (i.e., classroom lights flickering, the teacher raises her hand, etc.);
4. Entering the classroom (such as at the start of the day or after lunch, gym, recess, etc.).

You can teach your child to respond to these cues using physical prompts that are faded as quickly as possible. The teaching strategies are similar to what we described earlier—avoid verbal prompts, provide physical assistance preferably from behind your child, and provide positive outcomes that are as natural as possible. We arrange the pictures and symbols on the schedule in a vertical sequence (in part because we start schedules with very young children, including those who may have difficulty with right-left discrimination). Another option is to include one activity per page in a separate booklet. (See McClannahan and Krantz (1999), *Activity Schedules for Children* with *Autism: Teaching Independent Behavior*, Bethesda, MD: Woodbine House, for more details.)

See photo above for an example of an in-class schedule.

Understanding Changes in Routines and Expected Outcomes

Twelve-year-old Jeff was terrific at using his daily picture schedule. He came into class each morning and immediately checked for his first activity. However, his teacher found there to be one major problem. If something did not go EXACTLY as scheduled, Jeff would get very upset and usually would not proceed with his schedule. While his teacher was happy that Jeff had gained some independence, she was not pleased that he could not tolerate any change at all. It is one thing to try to perfectly control everything in the life of a three-year-old, but it is impossible to do so with a teenager. His teacher realized that no one had taught Jeff to tolerate the changes that occur in all our lives.

Here we see an example of how learning one lesson—following a picture schedule—can sometimes create new behavior management concerns—intolerance for changes in the schedule. Therefore, it is important to teach such tolerance as part of the overall strategy for all students rather than waiting to see which students develop similar problems. There are several ways that such lessons can be arranged.

The changes that children with autism encounter tend to range from things they like (e.g., going outside to play, working with my favorite teacher, etc.) to things that are not as much fun (e.g., staying indoors because it is raining, working with a substitute teacher who doesn't know me, etc.).

One simple strategy for teaching tolerance of changes is to systematically introduce changes that initially are "good" surprises. For example, in schedules we design, we include a symbol that stands for "surprise," often just a large question mark or even the word "surprise" on a uniquely colored and shaped background. When the children initially reach this point in their schedules, the teachers arrange for this "surprise" activity to involve lots of rewarding activities and treats. The "surprise" may be placed at any point in the schedule. At first, it often replaces work time or other less fun activities.

Over time, some of the "surprises" are activities that are less exciting. Finally, the surprises tend to be work-related changes. We make sure that the students are richly rewarded for participating in these activities. We want them to learn that the surprise picture might mean they have to do something that is immediately fun (e.g., party instead of work), or that the surprise activity will end in something wonderful just because they followed the schedule. It is important to keep providing some "surprises" that are highly interesting and motivating so that the children cannot predict which type of surprise comes next.

Once this mixture of "surprises" is part of the routine, when true surprises arise the teacher can now simply put the "surprise" symbol on the schedule and assume that the lesson will continue to work in these cases as well. Thus, our overall strategy is: "Since we all know that unexpected changes are part of life, why allow life to arrange for the lesson when teachers and parents can teach this lesson much more effectively?"

Understanding "Wait"

Ralph was nineteen years old and had successfully worked at a job in the community for the past several years. He seemed to enjoy his work but he most enjoyed going to get a hamburger at the end of each workday. Years earlier, he had displayed periodic episodes of extreme aggression but he had not attacked anyone for over a year. His teacher routinely took Ralph and another student on public transportation to their work site, as well as to their favorite hamburger location. One winter day, his teacher was walking with both students when the other student sneezed. The teacher assessed the situation and quickly surmised that she would need to return to class and clean the student's coat. She knew she still had plenty of time to get on the bus.

The teacher signaled to both students that they needed to return to the classroom. She thought she had conveyed that the young men would need to wait for a moment before returning to their activity. The next thing she knew, Ralph had head-butted her, nearly breaking a rib, and then started pounding her while she lay on the sidewalk. Why had he suddenly attacked her? Essentially, while she thought she had communicated for him to "wait," he thought she had communicated, "No, we are not going to get your favorite hamburger."

The long-term solution lay in developing a plan to teach Ralph how to wait, as well as to tolerate changes in expected routines. This type of training took over six months, but at the end of this period, the teacher was able to request that Ralph wait for an anticipated treat without any negative reaction.

Learning to wait can be a difficult lesson for many children. From one perspective, learning to wait can be viewed as related to a child's self-control or the ability to calmly handle delayed gratification. However, we can also view learning to wait as a communication issue, since children need to understand what we mean when we say, "Wait!" For example, once your child has learned to request her favorite snacks, she will eventually ask for the snack at a time when you do not have the snack with you. You are likely to say, "Wait! I'll go get it!" In such situations, it is important for your child to understand that "wait" is different than "no." When we say "wait" to a child, we have essentially made a promise, as in "I know what you want and you will get it, but you will get it somewhat later than you expected." How can we teach this complex lesson to children who have significant communication limitations?

The key to teaching someone to wait for an expected reward is for the teacher to be able to perfectly control access to the reward and the length of the waiting period. The need to control the duration of waiting from the beginning of training makes it difficult to teach this lesson in natural settings, such as at a fast-food restaurant. In such places, we do not know how long anyone will need to wait for the food. It also is helpful if we know precisely what a child would like to receive after waiting for a short time. Therefore, this "wait" lesson is best started after a child has learned to reliably ask for the things she likes. In addition, using a visual cue that is associated with "wait" makes it more likely that the child will understand our message.

For example, if a child requests a cookie (over which we have complete control) with PECS, we can take her picture (or sentence strip) and immediately give her a visual symbol for "wait" (and, if we like, say, "You need to wait"). Because a symbol that is naturally associated with "wait" is difficult to represent, we make a large, brightly colored sign with the word "WAIT" boldly printed (see picture on the next page). Whether the child actually reads the printed word or merely associates this unique symbol with "waiting" is not important at this point in training. While the child holds the wait-card (undoubtedly wondering what is going on!) the teacher silently counts to five seconds and then immediately says, "Nice waiting" while giving the child whatever was requested and taking back the wait-card. Over the next set of trials, the teacher gradually increases the length of time for the child to wait. Generally, such increases should be done in small enough increments that the child hardly notices the change from trial to trial.

Of course, no matter how gradually you increase the waiting time, at some point your child is likely to protest! In such cases, it is important to prevent her from succeeding in obtaining what she wants through actions associated with protesting (crying, screaming, grabbing, etc.). Do not give her the desired item, but wait for the protest to end. The next time, *decrease* the length of time your child needs to wait and then gradually lengthen the wait-period over subsequent opportunities.

As with other objectives, it is important to bear your child's age in mind when deciding how long she should wait. For example, asking any child under five to wait for more than five minutes can be expected to elicit a tantrum regardless of her disability!

Another important part of this training strategy is to recognize some of your own adult preferences for waiting and to incorporate these into the training. For example, if you were in a situation in which you knew you'd have to wait for a long time (e.g., you had a doctor's appointment at 3:00 but you knew for sure that you would *not* be seen at 3:00), you'd probably make sure you had something to do while waiting. That is, assuming you hate to wait and do nothing. You'd bring a book or something else to do, and if you forgot to bring something to read, there is always a magazine available—after all, the area where you wait is called "the waiting room!" Therefore, as your lesson on waiting proceeds with your child, you should make certain that she too has something to do while waiting for what she really wants. Some of the options that you should have available and encourage her to use include: playing with a simple toy, looking at a picture magazine, listening to music, etc.

Understanding Transitions

When Robin arrived at school, she often was upset upon stepping off the bus, even before staff had a chance to say anything to her. On such days, she often cried while walking to class. Once she was in the class, she generally calmed down after twenty or so minutes. Then the teacher would announce it was time for gym. Robin would fall down and cry once more, and do so all the way to the gym. After twenty or so minutes in gym, she'd usually calm down. Shortly after that, the teacher would announce that it was time to go back to class. Once again, Robin would start crying. During most of the transitions from one activity to another, Robin would cry and act out.

On the theory that perhaps Robin didn't understand what she was being told, the teacher began showing Robin pictures of the next activity. That is, while in class, the teacher showed Robin a picture of the gym, and while in gym, the teacher showed her a picture of the class she would be returning to. This strategy proved to be mildly helpful, but Robin continued to cry during most transitions.

Why did Robin continue to have problems with transitions even after the teacher added a visual cue to her communications? Quite frankly, this step is often all that is needed to help children with autism make successful transitions. That is, as we have noted, some children do not understand our spoken words and the addition of visual cues helps them comprehend our message. However, Robin seemed to need something more.

In addition to *how* we communicate, we must pay attention to *what* we communicate. In Robin's case, the teacher chose to communicate about the activity change and the location of the activity, perhaps because this is the type of information we adults would include in our daily schedule system. However, we believe that many children are focused on their reinforcers rather than their activities. If this interpretation is correct, then when we communicate to a child that they need to change activities (by telling them about the next activity) the child remains focused on her immediate reinforcer. For example, notice that prior to each transition, Robin was reasonably calm. She was likely engaged in some enjoyable action when the announcement came to change activities. If she were playing with crayons when she was told that it was time to go to gym, what Robin understood was that it was time to give up the crayons. Likewise, when she had calmed down enough in gym to finally begin playing with a ball, she heard that it was time to go back to class. To Robin, this message said, "It's time to give up the ball."

Whenever we have to give up a current reinforcer, we all act badly! Therefore, if Robin is focused on her reinforcers, then we should consider communicating about what Robin finds important. For example, while she is in the classroom, it would be more effective to communicate about the next reinforcer (the ball she enjoys in gym) than to communicate about the crayons she is going to have to give up. So, instead of announcing a change in activity, the teacher should approach Robin and signal the availability of the ball, via pictures or the actual object, if necessary. Such objects can be called "transitional objects." When Robin becomes focused on getting the ball, the teacher can calmly point out that we play with the ball in the gym. Rather than highlighting what Robin has to give up, this strategy emphasizes what Robin can get next.

While Robin is in the gym and playing with the ball, the teacher should approach her and communicate about the next reinforcer obtainable in the class: the crayons, snack time, music, etc. Robin will more readily give up the ball if she understands what she will gain by the change. In situations where there may not be a natural reward related to an activity, it will be important to arrange for something positive to happen for the child once the activity is completed. For example, although we may enjoy some aspects of our jobs, we do other aspects because we know we are going to get paid. This same strategy is important to use with children learning lessons (see the next section for more details).

This strategy of preparing children for transitions works equally well at home. We worked with one mother who liked to take her son for a walk after dinner. However, at some point, she would want to turn around and go home. When she would say, "Let's go home," her son would have a tantrum. Lengthening the walk would only postpone the inevitable screaming. When we discussed communicating about his reinforcers rather than her scheduled activity, the mother decided to change her routine. Now before they go for their walk, she has her son select a video (by taking the empty video cover) and she takes the cover on the walk. When she is ready to return, she simply takes out the video box. Her son knows that the VCR is at home and now leads the way back cheerfully!

Understanding and Using Visual Reinforcement Systems Or: Let's Make a Deal!

We all knew that Mindy loved to eat popcorn. Her teachers often used popcorn to motivate Mindy to attend to and complete her work. However, the teachers noticed that Mindy often seemed unsure of when she could simply ask for or take some popcorn and when she had to earn some popcorn. The teachers also were not sure how to communicate to Mindy just how much work she needed to do before having some popcorn. We asked her teachers how they knew how much work they needed to do before they got their paychecks, when they would get they pay, etc. They looked at us as if we were daft and said, "It's in our written contract!" We looked at them and simply said, "So?"

Mindy's teachers wanted her to understand that if she successfully completed her lesson, she would earn the popcorn that she liked. A great deal of communication is involved in this arrangement—the teacher must know what the child likes, the child must know what the teacher expects, the child also must know how much work will result in how big a reward. Our point to her teachers was that when they make a "deal" with their boss, they insist on visual representation of that deal—a written contract. As I've noted earlier, one of my guiding principles is that "if it's good for us, it's good for the kids." Can we introduce "Let's make a deal" in an effective manner that will help Mindy become a better student?

We can make a reasonable comparison between the teacher/student relationship and the worker/boss relationship. First, let's remember that in our culture, students attend schools because they must. We have truancy laws to assure their attendance. When they show up at school, what is expected of them? Well, the most fundamental thing that teachers want of their students is for the students to learn.

What does it mean to learn? In its simplest sense, to learn means to change behavior. As teachers, we would only know if our students learned a lesson if those students could do something differently after the lesson than they did before the lesson. Students can demonstrate their learning by saying something new (a new word, sentence or idea), or by doing something differently (answering a question on a multiple choice test, tying their shoes, opening a container, etc.). So, when children come to school they meet powerful adults who expect them to do something—to learn for the teacher. And who selects what will be learned? It is the teacher with input from parents who sets the curriculum. In what other relationship does a powerful person tell the less powerful individual what to do? One is the parent-child relationship, but the other is the worker-boss relationship, in which the boss wants the worker to do something—the job—for the boss.

How do we design an effective deal? Our employer wants us to do something—the job. We only agree to do the job if we know what we will get in exchange for working. There are several important factors in arranging our "deal" with our boss. First, we would not accept the job if the boss said, "OK, I want you to do this job for a year and then I'll let you know what you will be paid." We would only accept the position if we knew our salary before we started to work. Notice also that we, not the boss, pick the type of reward for work (not how much—it's never enough!). We also want to know when we will get paid—weekly, monthly, etc. Another critical aspect of our contract with our employer is specifying our benefits. One of the most important benefits is vacation time—my ability to tell my boss when I need some time off. Here, too, in typical contracts, we tell our employer when we will use our vacation days. Finally, as noted earlier, we insist that all aspects of our deal with our boss be put in writing—essentially providing a visual representation of our deal.

How can we design a system that will convey all of the same types of information to students with limited communication skills? First, it is important to remember that we select our own rewards and so too should the children. We can allow them to indicate their choice of reward simply by offering potentially rewarding items and observing what they reach for, or we can ask the child what she would like to work for, if she has the communication skills to reply.

We then teach the child how we use "Let's make a deal." Once she has requested a reward, we indicate, often with gestures, for her to do something that is very simple—something that we know she can already do. For example, when your child gives you a picture of a cookie as a request, you might point and gesture to a toy on the floor, prompting her to give it to you. When she gives you the toy, you would immediately give her the cookie while saying, "Nice work!"

Gradually, as your child becomes more skilled at using PECS to make requests, you would begin to require small tasks to be completed prior to giving her what she requests. This interaction is your deal. Of course, you would not react to every request your child makes by starting a "deal!" In kind, it's important (and kind-

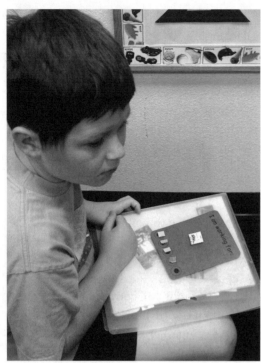

hearted) to occasionally give your child things she likes simply out of love—no one should have to earn everything! As the deals begin to require more work, there comes a point when your child may wonder what she is doing all this work for! At that point, you would put her picture icon on a separate card that states, "I am working for...." (or some similar phrase).

On this card is a single circle (usually containing a Velcro dot). Now, when your child completes the task you indicated, you immediately give her a token and show her how to place the token on the circle. This token is essentially the same as money that we are paid for doing our job. Since there is only one circle on the card, and it is filled with a token, the job is complete. Now you teach your child to "spend" her token; that is, she gives the token to you and you immediately give her what she originally requested.

Just as every employer fundamentally wants "more work, less pay," teachers and parents want students to do more work with less feedback over time—in other words, to become more independent. Therefore, when your child seems to understand the value of the single token, place a second circle on the work card. Now she can only cash in the tokens when both circles are filled with tokens. Then, sticking with the tradition of requiring more work, gradually add a third, a fourth, and eventually a fifth circle to the work card. At any point during the deal, the work card contains information about what your child can earn (i.e., the picture she used to make her request), information about how long the job lasts (i.e., it's a five-circle job), and how close she is to the next payday (depending on how many tokens are filling circles). It is important to start the system with just one circle—not the five that you hope to get to.

You also may want to place a "break" symbol on the work-card to remind your child that she can request a "vacation" at any time. Of course, just as with your own vacations, there are rules about how long the break will last, how many can be requested within some period of time, and what you can do on break. Unlike a vacation—where adults often try to go someplace very rewarding—a break from work (or school work) is simply a request to get away from the demanding situation for a short while. Thus, while we suggest having a break-area (certainly not the time-out area, if one is used!), we also suggest having only boring or mildly interesting things to do in that area. After all, we want to convince the child that it is more rewarding to complete the work than to sit in the break area!

As children mature, the deals stretch out and begin to resemble the work situation in which we all find ourselves. We typically work for a couple of hours and then find some time to grab a snack, chew some gum, get a drink, etc. As students enter the workforce, they too will need to be able to work for a couple of hours before getting to the things they really like. Visual contracts such as described here help children with autism know what they are working for, how long they will have to work, and how soon the next reward time will come. We never would totally eliminate the system, just as we do not eliminate our contract with our boss even after years of employment. The questions below should help guide you through designing comprehensive deals:

Questions Complete Contracts Must Answer
- Who picks the type of reward?
- Remember to first determine the reward, then place the demand.

- Can we renegotiate the deal?

The following elements must be visually signaled to the student:

- What am I working for? (Either the item itself, or, when possible, a picture or other symbol that represents the item, such as a picture from a reward menu or the child's PECS book.)
- How much work is needed to get the reward? (The number of open circles on a token-card, the number of puzzle pieces a card is cut into, etc.)
- How often do I get paid? (Cash-in times can be noted on the schedule board.)
- When is my next payday? (The child can tell by noting how many *open* circles are left on the token-card.)
- When can I take a break? (The "break" cards may even be placed on the reinforcer card.)
- What are the rules about my breaks?
- How many do I get? (This is set by the number of break-cards made available.)
- How long do they last? (Set a count-down timer—the child can set it too.)
- What can I do while I'm on break? (What magazines or other low-reward items are available in the break-area?)

If possible, visually depict the type of work to be done (e.g., math lesson, putting toys away, setting the table, going to gym, etc.)

Closing Remarks

Teaching children to be effective communicators is one of the most important and rewarding goals for professionals and parents alike. We all would like for our children to learn to speak well. However, as we have tried to stress throughout this book, children and adults who do not speak can still be excellent communicators. What these individuals need from us is patience to figure out what they want, skill to set up an effective training program, and flexibility to make thoughtful adjustments best suited to that person.

We hope that this book will spark interest in following up on many of the resource materials noted at the end of each chapter. The intent of this book is to provide you with assistance in making the first steps down a critical pathway. Our hope is that you will walk down that path hand in hand with the person you love or work with and then be able to let go of that hand when the time comes for independence. We hope you will find the many ways that our children can respond with expressions of their love for your efforts and dedication.

References & Resources

McClannahan, L. & Krantz, P. (1999). *Activity schedules for children with autism: Teaching independent behavior*, Bethesda, MD: Woodbine House.

RESOURCE GUIDE

PECS Training, Information, and Products

We (the authors) have formed a consulting group—Pyramid Educational Consultants, Inc.—to provide training and consultation regarding PECS and various teaching strategies appropriate for children and adults with autism and other disabilities. Pyramid Educational Consultants, Inc., provides workshops for professionals and parents designed to give people the necessary skills to start PECS. We also have a *certification* process that allows us to identify people who have demonstrated skills in implementing PECS, as well as those who have demonstrated skills in supervising others in the use of PECS. (If a member of your child's team is providing your PECS support, you may want to check on the type of training they have received. We understand that some people with whom we have had no contact will be able to provide competent consultation regarding PECS; however, we can only comment about those who have completed our certification process.) Families and programs may contact us at:

Pyramid Educational Consultants, Inc.
226 West Park Place, Suite 1
Newark, DE 19713
888-PECS-INC (888-732-7482) Toll free within the USA
302-368-2515 (international calls)
Web site: http://www.pecs.com (frequently updated)

We also have developed a number of products specifically designed to make PECS use more effective and efficient for children and teachers. Please contact:

Pyramid Educational Products, Inc.
5-C Garfield Way
Newark, DE 19713
302-894-9155
Web site: http://www.pyramidproducts.com

If you have questions regarding PECS in general (i.e., training, products, etc.), use in a program (school or agency based, in-home, etc.), or use with an individual, please feel free to contact Pyramid Educational Consultants by phone, email, or in writing. However you contact us, we will try to help you as best we can.

Applied Behavior Analysis

The Association for Behavior Analysis
213 West Hall
Western Michigan University
1201 Oliver St.
Kalamazoo, MI 49008
616-387-8341
http://www.wmich.edu/aba/index.html

Association for the Advancement of Behavior Therapy
305 7th Ave., 16th Floor
New York, NY 10001
212-647-1890
http://www.aabt.org

Behavior Analyst Certification Board
519 E. Park Ave.
Tallahassee, FL 32301
http://www.bacb.com

Autism and Communication Skills

American Speech-Language Hearing Association (ASHA)
10801 Rockville Pike
Rockville, MD 20852
800-638-8255
http://www.asha.org

Autism Society of America
7910 Woodmont Ave.
Suite 300
Bethesda, MD 20814
301-657-0881; 800-3-AUTISM (328-8476)
http://www.autism-society.org

Sources of Information and Equipment for AAC

AbleNet, Inc.
1081 Tenth Ave. N. E.
Minneapolis, MN 55414-1312
800-322-0956
http://www.ablenetinc.com

Closing the Gap
P. O. Box 68
Henderson, MN 56004.
612-248-3294
http://www.closingthegap.com

Communication Skill Builders
313 North Dodge Blvd., Box 42050-H
Tucson, AZ 85733
602-323-7500
http://www.psychcorp.com/catg

Crestwood Communication Aids
6625 North Sidney Place
Milwaukee, WI 53209
414-352-5678
http://www.communicationaids.com

Don Johnston, Inc.
26799 West Commerce Dr.
Volo, IL 60073
847-740-0749; 800-999-4660
http://www.donjohnston.com

Dynavox Systems, Inc.
2100 Wharton St.
Pittsburgh, PA 15203
888-697-7332
http://dynavoxsys.com

Imaginart
307 Arizona St.
Bisbee, AZ 85603
800-828-1376; 520-432-5741
http://www.imaginartonline.com

IntelliTools, Inc.
1720 Corporate Circle
Petaluma, CA 94954
800-899-6687; 707-773-2000
http://www.intellitools.com

ISAAC (International Society for Augmentative
and Alternative Communication)
49 The Donway West
Suite 308
Toronto, ON, M3C 3M9, Canada
416-385-0351
http://Isaac-online.org

Mayer-Johnson Company
P.O. Box 1579
Solana Beach, CA 92075
800-588-4548; 800-550-0084
http://www.mayer-johnson.com

Prentke Romich Company
1022 Heyl Road
Wooster, OH 44691
800-262-1933
http://www.prentrom.com

RESNA (Assoc. for the Advancement of Rehabilitation Technology)
1101 Connecticut Ave., NW, Suite 700
Washington, DC 20036
202-857-1140
http://www.resna.org

Sammons Preston
AbilityOne Corp.
4 Sammons Ct.
Bolingbrook, IL 60440
800-323-5547 (in U.S.); 800-665-9200 (in Canada)
http://www.sammonspreston.com

The U.S. Society for Augmentative and Alternative Communication
c/o Barkley Memorial Center
University of Nebraska
Lincoln, NE 68588
402-472-5463

Words+, Inc.
40015 Sierra Highway
Bldg. B-145
Palmdale, CA 93550
800-869-2521
http://www.words-plus.com

Zygo Industries, Inc.
P.O. Box 1008
Portland, OR 97207-1008
800-234-6006
http://www.zygo-usa.com

INDEX

ABOUT THE AUTHORS

Andy Bondy, Ph.D., has over thirty years experience working with children and adults with autism and related developmental disabilities. He served for over twelve years as the Director of the Statewide Delaware Autistic Program. He has taught numerous university level courses for teachers and specialists regarding autism, behavior analysis, curriculum design, effective instruction, and functional communication training. He has presented regional, national, and international workshops concerning educational, behavioral, and communicative issues pertaining to individuals with autism from preschool age through adulthood. He has assisted many schools around the world in improving their services for students with special needs. He designed the Pyramid Approach to Education as a comprehensive combination of broad-spectrum behavior analysis and functional communication strategies. He is co-developer of the Picture Exchange Communication System.

Lori A. Frost, M.S., CCC/SLP, is a speech-language pathologist certified by the American Speech-Language-Hearing Association. She has nearly twenty years experience working with children with limited communication and severely challenging behavior. She is co-developer of the Picture Exchange Communication System, a unique augmentative communication system that has been used widely with children and adults who have difficulty using speech as a primary mode of communication. She has led regional, national, and international conferences and workshops. She consults to numerous schools and programs worldwide regarding the development of functional communication skills for children and adults with autism and related disabilities.

Pat Mirenda, Ph.D., has been an Associate Professor in the Department of Educational and Counselling Psychology and Special Education at the University of British Columbia (UBC) since September 1996. Dr. Mirenda lectures widely and teaches UBC courses about inclusive education, developmental disabilities, autism, augmentative communication, and supporting students with behavior problems in schools. The second edition of her book, *Augmentative and Alternative Communication: Management of Severe Communication Disorders in Children and Adults,* was published in May 1998. Her current research includes a three-year evaluation of the outcomes of intensive early intervention on young children with autism and their families.